TRACKS IN THE DUST

By the same author:

To a Land He Showed Us
In the Tanganyika Bush
Amid Perils Often

TRACKS IN THE DUST

Stanley W. Hoffman

VANTAGE PRESS
New York

Scriptural quotes in this book are from the New International Version of the Bible.

FIRST EDITION

All rights reserved, including the right of
reproduction in whole or in part in any form.

Copyright © 1996 by Stanley W. Hoffman

Published by Vantage Press, Inc.
516 West 34th Street, New York, New York 10001

Manufactured in the United States of America
ISBN: 0-533-11674-0

Library of Congress Catalog Card No.: 95-90650

0 9 8 7 6 5 4 3 2 1

To my wife,

Marion Margaret,

who in Africa has walked faithfully at my side

in most places where I have walked

I will give you every place where you set your foot, as I promised Moses.
—Joshua 1:3

Contents

Preface	xi
Introduction	xiii
Chapter One. My Wife	1
Chapter Two. Healings	9
Chapter Three. More Healings	18
Chapter Four. A Regrettable Incident	27
Chapter Five. Nighttime Adventures	35
Chapter Six. Thefts	43
Chapter Seven. He Will Provide	63
Chapter Eight. Signs and Wonders	70
Chapter Nine. Miracles	82
Chapter Ten. The Complexities of Marriage	92
Chapter Eleven. Recollections	104
Chapter Twelve. The Wagusii	116
Chapter Thirteen. The Lost Keys	126
Chapter Fourteen. The Stoning	147
Chapter Fifteen. Female Circumcision	154
Chapter Sixteen. A Dream Fulfilled	162
Chapter Seventeen. Away from the Crowds	171
Chapter Eighteen. Hunting Safaris	182
Chapter Nineteen. Farewell, Africa!	193
Chapter Twenty. What Next?	202

Preface

This book is a sequel to my earlier book, *To a Land He Showed Us*. It concludes our years spent in Tanzania (formerly Tanganyika), experiences not previously mentioned in the above book. As well you will read of our move from our beloved people in Tanzania to Kenya and the adventures that followed while we were serving the Lord in that East African country.

Let me take you back there with me! In order to help you to be a part of our lives at the time they happened, I am writing, as in my other books, in the present tense. May you be blessed while reading about them now as we were blessed as they happened then.

Introduction

Marion and I have returned to visit Mbugwe, where we lived for fifteen years. It has been twenty years now since we moved away from here. The sun is still as hot as we remember it back then. There has been no rain for so long that every bush and blade of dry grass is coated with dust. Our shoes are covered with the stuff! Dust devils spiral across the flats. Heat waves shimmer, and there is a mirage. The blue escarpment against the western skyline is still as picturesque as ever.

Even as I look at it today, I am reminded again of Psalm 121. As rugged as that Rift Wall is, it is no match to the strength given by the Lord. How often I depended on His supernatural strength to survive in this land. And survive we did.

We have met many of our old friends. A few of them are no longer around. They have passed over to the other side. Marion and I move from hut to hut and chat with those who remember us still. It is good to see them again. At Mwada we find Matea, whose son was sacrificed by the witch doctor in order to induce rainfall. This happened during our stay in Mbugwe. Just previous to this incident, Maria narrowly escaped a similar fate, which I have shared in my previous book *To a Land He Showed Us* in chapter 8. Romonah reminds us that Matea's son was the last person to be sacrificed for rain here in Mbugwe. (Eliezer Mdobi and his wife have been driving us around in their vehicle today.)

The mission station we built at Kaiti no longer serves them. When missionaries no longer wished to live there, out in the African bush, the potash mining company at Minjingu took it over, and their staff resided there until recently, when the wildlife department moved in with their game scouts. When Marion and I put our roots down here back in 1959, we never dreamed that it would turn out this way!

As we look at it today, memories of our stay flood over us. The buildings we erected and the trees we planted with loving care are mostly still here. Monkeys scurry off the plot as we wander about. Elephants have stripped off all the greenery from the mango trees. They still come as they used to in search of water in the riverbed where leopards, we are told, still prowl.

A gust of wind twists by me as I gaze at the huts and the people of Mbugwe. It scoops up the fine volcanic dust and turns it over and over. The tracks we had made coming here are almost wiped away. There should be other tracks as well around here that Marion and I made on previous occasions when we walked from hut to hut visiting the Christians and praying for the sick. And there should be those of our vehicle as we sped across the flats on our way to a distant church. That really churned up the white dust! One could see it for miles.

My eyes rove to and fro searching, almost frantically. They are not really gone, are they? I want very much to see those tracks again as they bring back so many unforgettable memories of signs, wonders, and miracles we had in Mbugwe. I keep searching, looking out onto the flats. And, gradually, the tracks in the dust commence to appear one by one. And I remember . . .

Stanley W. Hoffman
Mbugwe, Tanzania
July 1994

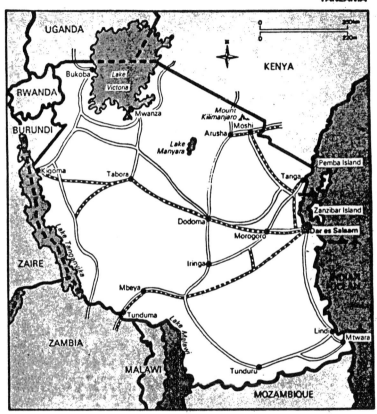

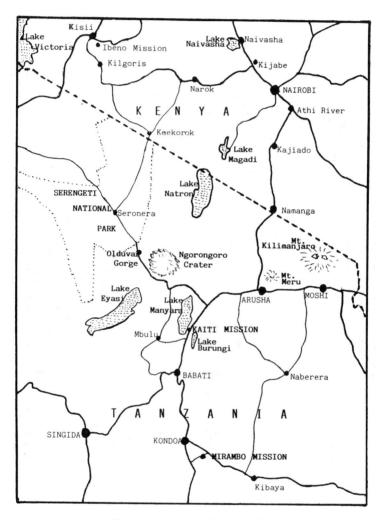

Places where we left our tracks

TRACKS IN THE DUST

Chapter One

My Wife

I first met my wife, then Marion Schwartz, in January 1956 at Camrose, Alberta. I had enrolled a term earlier at the Alberta Bible Institute or ABI (now Gardner Bible College) and was there when she arrived to take a few more courses in order to better equip her for the mission field. She had been there a few years ago and graduated with a Christian education diploma. But now she was here on a quest to prepare herself to be a missionary.

Marion was born in Neidpath, a very small village in southwestern Saskatchewan near Swift Current. It was on June 6, 1931, that she entered the lives of Alexander and Lydia Schwartz. There were five children who survived the hardships of those early years on the windswept prairies of western Canada. Marion was the second child in the Schwartz family, after Eileen, her sister. Then followed three brothers: Edwin, John, and Jerry. There were two others, but they died either at birth or soon after.

Marion recalls that they were poor but always had something to eat on their farm. Even though her dad was weary from his work, he would get down on the floor and give the children a ride on his back after the evening chores were done. She has fond memories of climbing on his lap and being cuddled and comforted by him. His nickname for her was Suzi, which she kept until his passing.

While Marion was still a preschooler, the parents moved to the Okanagan Valley in British Columbia. Grandfather Schwartz had moved there earlier and probably was now the cause of Alexander's hankering to take his family there as well. But it was short-lived. Soon they found themselves back on the old farm in Saskatchewan.

Marion has some recollection of that brief stay in British Columbia. One day, when she and Edwin were sent by their mother to deliver an axe to Aunt Esther's, they had to try it out as soon as they were out of sight. Edwin said, "Let's chop some wood. You put it down and hold it while I chop." So he did just that, right on Marion's head! She could not comb her hair for some time.

Another incident took place soon after. While Marion was recovering from the cut on her head, she and Edwin were playing with their wagon outside. Telephone men were digging holes in the vicinity for the poles. It had rained recently and the holes were now partially full of water. While Edwin was pulling the wagon and Marion pushing, they crossed over one of the holes and she dropped down into it. She nearly drowned before her mother rescued her.

Edwin decided then he would be nice to his sister. Since their mother would not let them go outside, he was going to push Marion around on the tricycle. There was a potbellied heater in the room, and it was red-hot. The two were cruising right along, laughing and enjoying themselves. Then the trike tipped and Marion fell against the hot stove, burning both hands severely! She had to be fed for some time. Guess by whom? Yes, Edwin.

She remembers walking to school in her early years at Neidpath catching a ride in the horse-drawn cart that her sister used in delivering milk. Marion found school a disappointment because she had to sit still at a desk and was not able to talk. So she looked for excuses and invented all kinds of sicknesses, so as not to go to classes. But it usually didn't work. When her brother Edwin started school it became more bearable for her. Now it was double trouble! Because of their mischievousness they were known as Hans and Fritz, the Katzenjammer Kids.

After she completed her grade school (her high school she did later), she entered the workforce. At seventeen she found herself working as the secretary at the town office in Neidpath. She was in charge of the books and collecting taxes. There was a bounty on for coyotes, she recalls, and when they brought in their ears she would pay them the money. For gopher tails as well. There usually was not much to do, since it was not a big town. There was a Bible on her desk in front of her that was used for swearing in district officers and councillors. She often was tempted to read it.

One day, when her work was completed for the day, she picked up the Bible and opened it to Proverbs, chapter 10. She read it and was convicted of her sins. In that public office, not caring who might enter, she then knelt at her chair and asked the Lord to save her. He did and she was filled with joy at her newfound salvation. While she was on her knees praying, God placed a call in her heart to be a missionary to Africa!

Marion discovered when she reached home that her mother had been fasting and praying for her. She was now overjoyed to hear of her daughter's decision to follow Christ. They both made a covenant to pray together for Marion's dad's and the other children's salvation. The Lord heard and honored their prayers and sacrifice. All of them accepted Christ at a revival meeting six months later! Others were saved through Marion's witnessing for Christ.

She worked one more year in the municipal office and then resigned to go off to ABI to join her brother Edwin, who had gone there a year earlier. At this time, while Marion was at Bible school, her parents moved to British Columbia again.

This time it was to stay and settle at Vernon in the Okanagan Valley. During each summer holiday, she worked at various jobs: tailoring, dry-cleaning, and waiting tables. At the end of four years she graduated with a Christian education diploma.

But something else had taken place in her life. She had let her call slip into the background. Instead of preparing for Africa, Marion took the job of a financial secretary and credit manager at the Hudson's Bay Company, a big department store in Vernon. She loved this kind of work and soon was buying the best kind of clothing. Also, she bought a bedroom suite, stainless steelware, silverware, bone china, luggage, etc. And always the best! She had become very materialistic.

Then, two years later, the brother who had been very close to her was killed at the family lumber mill. The saw caught the edge of a two-by-six and flung it, striking Edwin in the back of his neck while he had his head turned. It killed him instantly. That night Marion heard from God and He reminded her of the call to Africa. She struggled but finally yielded herself to Him and said "Yes, Lord," to His will as she had done years earlier. Four months later found her back at ABI.

It was difficult for us to miss one another during the day as we sat across the table from each other at mealtime. Marion appeared to be more mature spiritually than the girls I had dated previously. She, of course, had other ideas of me. She thought I was too noisy, to begin with, and could not get used to my singing as I ran up and down the stairs in my cowboy boots. But she finally relented and we soon were ice-skating together and even out strolling in the cold, wintery air. We did not mind, as the love bug had bitten us!

The rules at the school did not allow dating on campus. Marion and I reserved it for the weekends when we went out on gospel teams where a chaperon was present. I proposed to Marion on our way back to ABI from a hockey game where I had been hit in the face by a flying puck. She felt sorry for me, I guess, and said yes. I gave her the ring when she returned from the choir tour in April. I pulled her into chapel when no one was around and slipped the diamond on her finger. We told the president, Thomas Hall, and that evening in the dining hall he surprised everyone, except us, by announcing our engagement.

Marion returned to Vernon while I stayed on for the third term. During the midterm break I lit out for Vernon to see my sweetheart. I took the train and when I hit Kamloops, Marion was there with a vehicle to pick me up and drive me the rest of the way. I had as yet not met her parents. I wondered how they would receive me. Her father had consented to her marrying me when I wrote him earlier. Marion had often mentioned to me that he was a stern man and had been tough with her previous boyfriends when they came calling.

Well, here I was! Before Marion could usher me inside, her mother appeared at the door. She was friendly and invited me to come in. I did not see Marion's father anywhere. Where was he? I headed for the bathroom to check if I was presentable enough for my future father-in-law. I was dressed in green trousers, a wine shirt, and a yellow jacket. Just as I entered the bathroom, he was on his way out. We almost collided! With a quick smile and a short "Hello" from both of us, he kept going and I ducked inside and closed the door. That was not the way I had planned it!

We were finally properly introduced to each other, and all was well. I was so different from all her previous suitors that he found me a breath of fresh air. I had no trouble in communicating with him, and we became the best of friends. Marion's mother was, of course, a jewel. She won me over almost immediately. I now had found some parents again after a period of years without.

Because of the distance, only my sister, Doreen, and her

fiance, Allan Kramer (whom she later married), showed up from the prairies for our wedding on the eighteenth of August in 1956. For our honeymoon we spent a week at a guest ranch in the Caribou Mountains of British Columbia, followed by another week at Jasper, Alberta. I got in some horseback riding, which I love, at both places. Marion preferred walking or trolling for fish from a boat on a quiet lake with only the call of the loon to break the silence.

In fall we returned to ABI, where I continued my studies. Marion was hired on as the school secretary-treasurer. Her salary helped to pay for my textbooks and other incidentals. The payments from the sale of my father's farm took care of the school fees. In my third year Marion was expecting our first child. We decided then to take a pastorate after I graduated with my diploma in ministerial theology at the end of the third term. This we did and accepted the call to pastor the church at Schuler in southeastern Alberta.

Before we got there, though, Colleen was born on the first day of July 1958 in Vernon. She now accompanied us to the village of Schuler. The parsonage was in town, but the church was five miles out in the rolling countryside, surrounded by sprawling ranches. The congregation made us feel welcome, and we immediately felt at home among these suntanned and wind-burned ranchers. They showered us with meat and dairy products, so much so that we were never without. The winter was cold, with a lot of wind, snowdrifts piling up outside as high as the windowsill.

During this time at Schuler, preparations for our eventual departure for Africa gained momentum. Since our call to Africa as a couple, we had been praying earnestly for a door to open so that we could go. The call had come during a missionary service we attended at Camrose while in our last year at ABI. Frank La Font had been the missionary speaker. The burden for the souls in Africa gripped me. I had always had an interest in that continent and now it had increased to become a call. Marion had hers renewed, and we both accepted the challenge.

The truth finally sank in that the way we would be going was independently of our missionary board! We had inquired but were told to take more studies and then wait. The burden was too great to postpone it that far into the future. But would we have sufficient faith to take us there and then to sustain us in a strange land? The Word kept on reminding us that He would go with us and never forsake us.

Another couple in nearby Medicine Hat was also making plans to go to Africa as faith missionaries. They were Ralph and Gertie Farmer, who felt called to Kenya. They also had a small daughter; her name was Sherrie. He had been in contact with Twyla Ludwig, who was travelling the States for funds. She had invited all of us to stay at their station near Nairobi in Kenya until the time when the Lord revealed to us our own niche in Africa.

Marion began to feel the pangs of leaving the comforts of home. She must give it all up now. She turned to the Word for comfort. The Lord showed her the following passage of Scripture in Matthew 6:25–34:

Therefore I tell you, do not worry about your life, what you will eat or drink, or about your body, what you will wear. Is not life more important than food, and the body more important than clothes? Look at the birds of the air, they do not sow or reap or store away in barns, and yet your heavenly Father feeds them. Are you not much more valuable than they? Who of you, by worrying can add a single hour to his life? And why do you worry about clothes? See how the lilies of the field grow. They do not labor or spin. Yet I tell you that not even Solomon in all his splendor was dressed like one of these. If that is how God clothes the grass of the field, which is here today and tomorrow is thrown into the fire, will he not much more clothe you, O you of little faith? So do not worry, saying, "What shall we eat?" or "What shall we drink?" or "What shall we wear?" For the pagans run after all of these things, and your heavenly Father knows that you need them. But seek first his kingdom and his righteousness, and all these things will be given to you as well. Therefore do not worry about tomorrow, for tomorrow will worry about itself. Each day has enough trouble of its own.

She began to stand on this portion of His Word and would continue to do so even after we were in Africa.

The time arrived when we said farewell to the congregation at Schuler and travelled back to Vernon, where we made our final preparation for departure. The vehicle was sold, the money to be used to purchase one in Africa. Taking leave of her mother and father was not easy for Marion. But God gave her the grace and strength she needed.

Chapter Two
Healings

Africa can be hard on you. Always she demands watchfulness and full attention. Not only for the snakes that lie along the path, behind rocks, or on limbs of trees, but for the parasites as well that breed in the water you bathe with and in the water you drink. These microscopic bugs take a large toll of human life. I would much rather face a mean old buffalo with a rifle in my hand than a throng of mosquitoes with a flyswatter. The odds are that I would stand a much better chance of coming out unscathed with the former.

A survey in Mbugwe revealed that over 50 percent of the people have bilharzia. By drinking water collected from stagnant pools without boiling it first, they contract this killer disease. Water is safer from their wells, where the snail that carries this parasite cannot readily dwell. Another disease easily contracted from unboiled and unfiltered water or from eating unwashed fruit and vegetables is amoebic dysentery. If not treated in time, it, too, can be fatal, especially to children.

We have to learn to boil all the water for drinking, then run it through a filter and finally cool it in our kerosene fridge. In this hot climate that we have here it takes a lot of hustling to keep enough cold water around to keep our thirst quenched. Vegetables and fruits have to be washed in a solution containing bleach. In spite of the many precautions we take, the unavoidable happens. Africa waits her time. She has much more patience than we. When we forget she does not.

Only a few months after our arrival in Tanganyika, Marion contracts the uncomfortable disease amoebic dysentery. We are still in one of the houses at Bonga. Water from the rain cistern beside the house has not been sufficiently boiled. The common run of treatment does not cure her illness. There are times it goes into remission, but only to flare up again shortly after. Each time it is worse than before.

The roads we travel on are bumpy, full of holes, and corrugated. There is no tarmac to relieve the monotonous jolting of the vehicle as we journey over the many miles. Marion hangs on as best as she can, but often it is not enough. She bounces all the way up and hits her head on the roof. One second she is on the seat, the next second she is on her way up (no seat belts in those days). There are times she stays home, as the pain she has been experiencing recently in her abdomen worsens on rough roads.

The disease lingers on. She loses weight and becomes weaker. What normally should have taken only a few weeks to cure stretches into months and then years in spite of medical treatment and prayer. It is now three grueling years that she has been plagued with the illness. Then when her weight drops down to only ninety pounds, I make plans to take Marion to be checked by a specialist in Nairobi. There surely must be a cure for her ailment!

The specialist, a British doctor, calls me into his office after examining Marion thoroughly. He tells me bluntly that if I love her, I will take her away from East Africa. He goes on to say that she needs to move to a cold climate so that she can recuperate. Staying on in the tropics will not solve her problem, only continue to worsen it. She is severely inflamed and infected. When he discovers that we hail from Canada, he advises me that this is the ideal place for her to go to immediately.

Another problem that has developed because of her prolonged weakened state is a sagging of the bowels. They are now resting on her pelvis. On an X ray he shows me where one section of it is kinked, saying that any more travelling on rough roads could cause a strangulation of the intestine. (This is what is giving her such pain when the journeys get bumpy.) Should this happen, then toxic waste would back up into her system and death would follow.

The doctor recommends that Marion wear a wide belt for support until she leaves the country. It will be unbearably hot and uncomfortable, but there is no alternative. Or there is one, but not feasible. That is to have an operation where her insides would be tied up into place internally. For this kind of surgery Marion would have to enter a hospital in Texas where the doctor knew they could do it.

Needless to say, we leave his office all shaken up! Did the Lord call us to Tanganyika to serve Him for just three years? Has our time really come to leave? Somehow it all does not add up or make much sense. We have merely begun and many more years are still needed to establish the work in Mbugwe and Uburunge. But, I cannot endanger my wife's welfare any longer. We have prayed many times for her healing. Our missionary friends also have. There were times we saw some improvements, but they lasted for only a few days. Is this the Lord's way of saying that we should go home?

Travelling back to our station in Tanganyika, we decide to give God another chance to heal Marion before formulating our plans of returning home to Canada. If He wants us to stay on, He will have to perform a miracle. Otherwise, we will leave and seek the help of doctors.

When we arrive at Kaiti, we quickly compile a newsletter

requesting earnest prayer for Marion's affliction. It is then sent home to our supporters.

Upon receiving our letter, Marion's mother in Vernon, British Columbia, takes a handkerchief to church and asks those who believe in healing to step forward, lay their hands on the cloth, and help pray for her daughter's illness. The mother pours out her soul before the throne of God on behalf of her daughter in faraway Africa. The handkerchief is then sent to us.

We receive it the day we happen to have our missionary colleagues visiting us. After Marion and I share the letter with them, they gather around Marion with me. The anointed handkerchief is placed on her head, and we pray the prayer of acceptance. I receive a witness that healing is taking place. Marion feels it as well. And it is so!

The amoebic dysentery that has plagued her for three years ceases, and the pain in her abdomen leaves her. She is again able to travel with me to our churches. Praise the Lord!

When Marion is x-rayed on a later date, the bowels are observed to be in their normal position! God had performed a miracle! "Now, why did He not do this any sooner?" you might ask. Why wait for three years? All I know is that it was a greater testimony to the Christians in the homeland and in Tanganyika the way it turned out. Had Marion been healed soon after contracting this disease, not many would have heard of it. But now, not only did countless believers praise God for His power; they also had a part in asking God for her healing. They learned that intercessory prayer does move the hand of God! Especially a mother's prayer.

*　　*　　*

I might add that during her weakened state with amoebic dysentery, Marion carried our second child the full nine months and delivered a healthy boy, a little skinny, but a welcome sight nonetheless, on July 8, 1961, in the hospital at Arusha. I had slept in the car outside as Kirk Randall took his time in making his entrance. We had rushed the seventy-five miles to Arusha from Kaiti when Marion began labor pains. But it wasn't until the following day that she gave birth.

From the very beginning, mother and son have a rough time of coping with the hot climate in Mbugwe. To make matters worse, we are still living in the tin building, our first house on Kaiti Mission Station. The aluminum roof reflects some of the rays from the sun, but the tin walls make up for it by attracting the heat. It is unbearably hot inside at midday. During these times Marion will take Kirk and sit in the shade of our big fig tree in a reclining chair I have especially bought for them. Colleen keeps them company. And so do the monkeys who are above in the branches dining on the wild fruit. Eventually the children have one of them for a pet.

The year that Kirk is born, a drought is in progress of which I have shared in the last book, *To a Land He Showed Us,* in chapter 8. The Wambugwe quickly give him the name Njala, which in their language means "drought" or "hunger."

The heat and the bright aluminum roof make it more difficult for Kirk when he contracts German measles at eight months. He suffers greatly during this time and wants to be held continually. Because of the bright sun, he cannot be taken outside. So mother and son have to endure a lot during this time. And as I mentioned earlier, Marion is still afflicted with amoebic dysentery.

*　　*　　*

When I first met Marion she had a pair of glasses. She did not like to wear them all the time, but if she wanted to see things at a distance she had to put them on. She found them a nuisance after we got to Africa and tried not to wear them. But when she did this, she discovered she would get headaches, often quite severe, more like migraines. So she had no choice but to wear the glasses more often than not.

Through the years her farsightedness steadily decreases. Without her glasses she fails to recognize those we know as we pass by them on the road in our vehicle. I must tell her ahead of time when to wave so that her friends will not think that she is stuck-up. Then there are times she waves at a stranger, thinking that he or she is someone she knows. While viewing animals in the park, or just out on a drive near our mission station, Marion will hear one of our children inevitably say, "Mom, can't you see that impala? It's right beside that tree!" She has again left her glasses at home.

One day Marion receives a letter from a dear friend in the States who shares how the Lord had just healed her eyes! The lady went on to testify of how she had stood on the Word of God until He answered her prayer. It happens the day she goes to renew her driver's license. When it comes time to read the eye chart, she puts her faith into action by attempting it without her glasses. She discovers she is able to read it all the way down to the fine print! She no longer needs glasses.

After reading the letter, Marion is convicted and asks, "Where is my faith? Is the Lord a respecter of persons? Can I not trust Him for my healing too?" She begins to tell her friends that she is expecting God to heal her eyes. To assist her with a positive confession, she searches the Scriptures, as the Lord did say He would teach us. She stands on the verse found in Isaiah. 53:5: "By His stripes we *are* healed" and on the one in 1 Peter 2:24: "By His stripes you *have been* healed."

Every day Marion praises the Lord for her healing. But nothing happens. Then one day He speaks to her heart: *Why are you still hanging onto your glasses? Are you afraid I will not heal you?* Immediately she takes her glasses and throws them down our outhouse. When I hear this I have to admit that she is going the second mile!

When Satan comes to admonish her for throwing away such expensive glasses, Marion asks the Lord for a Scripture verse. He gives her Isaiah 49:23: "They shall not be ashamed that wait for me." She reads in Psalms 31:1: "In thee, O Lord, do I put my trust, let me never be ashamed." Then she receives another promise from the Lord. It is in Joel 2:27: "My people shall never be ashamed." He nudges her to confess her healing, to step over the side of the boat as Peter did.

That very day she comes to me and says, Stan, do you know that I can see? That is the moment that Marion receives her healing! For when she goes outside she is able to see the branches of trees and small tufts of grass in the distance. She is even able to spot some animals grazing out in the palm forest. Previously they were just a blur without her glasses. She has received new sight! Now she can say with the man at the pool of Siloam, "I can see! I can see!" Praise God!

Not only does Marion have her full sight restored, but the Lord also heals her of some other annoyances, one of them her migraine headaches. She discovers that He is more than enough! Through it all she has learned that it is true what is written in Romans 4:21: "Be fully assured that what God had promised, He was able also to perform." And as well in Hebrews 11:6: "He is a rewarder of them that diligently seek Him."

* * *

In my previous book I shared how I was healed of my hay fever in an unusual way. Now I wish to share how I was healed of another ailment, again in an unusual way.

The most agonizing of all pains I have ever had hits me one day, and I am prostrated. There is a stabbing sensation in the upper part of my abdomen in the right side. Any movement, however slight, causes me unbearable pain! I can only be absolutely still on my back. It isn't long before I have a fever. What is it? Nothing like this has happened to me before.

Malaria I have had many times. It has been my companion too often. Twice I was delirious in advanced stages. But this attack I now have is not malaria. Whatever it is, we must do what we have always done when ill, and that is to ask God for healing. Marion calls in those in the mission compound to lay on hands and pray for me. They crowd around the bed and offer up a prayer for my healing. I break out into a sweat even before they have removed their hands. And by the time they leave, the pain has subsided. What a relief! I am on my feet soon afterwards. Praise the Lord!

Several days later, I describe the symptoms of my illness to a missionary friend in Arusha. He replies that he had a similar attack a few weeks ago and when examined by the doctor was told that he has gallstones. So that is it! The attack I had several days ago was due to gallstones. I am feeling okay so I do not go for an examination immediately but promise myself to do so when next we visit our mission doctor in Kenya. We are long overdue with our annual physicals. The missionary board requires us to have physical examinations each year, but we just are not used to having one that often. Before we came under the board, we never had one during those nine years.

During those months of waiting, Marion discovers a concoction in a juice book that can dissolve gallstones. (It is amazing how the Lord shows you these things when you are in need!) Daily I drink the juice she prepares for me from vegetables. The taste is nothing to brag about, but I gulp it down as prescribed.

When I finally am examined by the doctor at Mwihila Hospital, he discovers no trace of any gallstones! Tests and X rays have revealed that all is well. Now, was it really a gallstone attack I had? If not, what was it? If it was, then God healed me. Or was it the juice? I will leave it up to you to decide. As for me, I know I have been healed through prayer and cured through natural vegetable juice! And you know what? I have not had another attack like that since! Thank you, Lord.

Chapter Three
More Healings

Marion and I are on foot walking to a low flat-roofed hut (called *tembe* in Swahili) out on the Mbugwe flats. Dust is swirling about us, and the sun is unbearably hot as usual. We have been summoned to the home of Chembe, a crippled girl of about twelve or thirteen. No one here seems to know their age, let alone the day of their birth. One can only guess. Should the baby be born during the rainy season, then his or her name will be Mvula (Rain). And if it happens to be during the dry season, then the name is sure to be Njala (Drought or Hunger).

This method of giving names gives some historical background to the time of the year the person was born. Then there are names that describe more the situation at hand. Should there be an elephant raiding their crops during this time, the baby will be named Tembo (Elephant). Likewise, if a hyena was howling outside the hut at the time of delivery, then the child's name is Fisi (Hyena). Many names are an embarrassment to the individual. So we find many choosing Biblical names when they are baptized. This is not a requirement on our part, but it is entirely their request.

We have begun holding services at Kaiti Village here on the alkaline flats near Lake Manyara. We are meeting in front of the low flat-roofed hut belonging to Chembe's parents. This home was chosen because of Chembe's mother having accepted Christ earlier during one our visits. The mother now wished for her family, and neighbours to hear about the Saviour and accept Him as she had done. That is why Marion and I are on our way to Chembe's home today. She had heard me preach on Sunday on the miracles that Christ had performed.

Mtaiko, the father of Chembe, is a popular diviner in the area. Those who have been bewitched come to him for help. Because Chembe cannot walk, the father is displeased with her. She will never grow up to be someone's wife. He has no hope of ever getting any dowry for her. Chembe is a complete loss to him! Why even have her? It would be better if she would die. He places her out in the hot sun each day, draping her across some poles beside the hut. There she will hang until someone removes her into the shade.

Hanging there in the burning heat, Chembe often wishes that she could die. There is no future for her. The father wants her dead. The mother cares but has no way of helping her escape the plight that she is in. How much Chembe really suffers no one will ever know, only Chembe herself. That is why she wishes to die.

She receives a glimmer of hope when she hears several choruses in her own language sung the last few weeks in front of her home. The missionaries who have moved into the area have been sharing of a God Who loves and cares for everyone. Then she hears the missionary speak of Jesus, who healed the sick when He was here on earth. Why, He even healed the lame! Chembe now wonders if this Jesus would heal her? The missionary has just said that Jesus will save whoever believes in Him from his or her sins. Likewise, if anyone is sick, He will heal that one if the person believes.

How Chembe wants to believe that! She musters up some courage and sends word to the missionary to come and help her to believe.

As we stand in front of the hut, the mother quickly fetches three-legged stools for us to sit on. Then she disappears inside to announce to her daughter that we have arrived. There is someone on either side of Chembe when they bring her out and seat her in front of us. She is pretty in spite of the large slash across each cheek, the tribal marking of the Wambugwe. Her eyes are sad, though the hurt cannot only be seen but also felt. Surely Christ came to save and heal such a one as her.

I share the gospel message, taking time to explain His love for her. She accepts Jesus as her personal Saviour. I want so much for Him to also heal her. So does she. So Marion and I lay our hands on her frail body and pray for her healing: "O God, straighten her limbs; bring life into them. Let her walk as others do. May she grow up to serve You. Heal her, Lord!" Before we leave we commit her into His hands and encourage her to keep believing that He has heard our prayer for her healing.

Several days later, Marion hears a *"Hodi?"* ("May I come in?") outside the kitchen door. Going to answer, she discovers a girl standing with a small bundle in her hands. The girl says, "Do you not know me? I am Chembe, the girl you prayed for that God would heal." It is she! She has walked all the way from her home, nearly two miles away, without anyone accompanying her. God has healed her! He has honoured her faith and answered our prayer. Praise the Lord!

Chembe goes on to say that she has come to work for Mama. She wishes to show her gratitude to us and to God and does not want any pay. She is eager to learn more about Christ and His ways. Her desire is to live for Him and to serve Him. We, of course, keep her, and she is employed to work for us. Florence, who helps Marion with the housework, will now have an assistant.

During the four years that Chembe is with us, she learns to bake, sew, wash clothing with a machine, and do many other things around the house. She remains faithful to the Master, ever thankful for His removing her from a crippled state. She has become physically healthy, and many young men wish to marry her. The father who had thought that he would never receive any cows for her now has many offers. Mtaiko accepted Christ into his life when he saw his daughter healed. How could he refuse someone so great?

Chembe becomes Elizabeth, the Biblical name she has chosen at baptism. She is a beautiful and radiant Christian. The man who finally wins her hand in marriage is the district youth leader. Many attend the Christian wedding in the church. They gather for the reception at her parents' home, the place where she had hung on the poles in the blistering heat waiting for death and where Christ had reached out and saved her and where He had healed her!

*   *   *

When Marion and I first arrived in Africa, we stayed for six weeks at Ruraka Mission just outside Nairobi. John and Twyla Ludwig had started a girls' domestic science school after having been retired by the missionary board. They wished to end their lives in Kenya, the land they had served as missionaries for many years.

During this time we meet many girls there, two of whom were to join us eventually in Tanganyika as house help. They are Florence and Romonah. The latter immediately attaches herself to us, especially to Colleen, our twelve-month-old baby. Romonah carries her around and washes our clothes in the open tubs on the compound. Just a super girl! When Colleen contracts dysentery, Romonah is there to assist Marion in baby-sitting.

Soon after the arrival of the Baums to assist us with the work in Tanganyika, Romonah comes to be their house girl.

She is an asset to the work of God as well with her radiant testimony of what the Lord means to her. Her father is an evangelist in the Church of God in Kenya and makes several visits to see his daughter at Kaiti. While with us, he is an inspiration to the church in Mbugwe. They all fall in love with him as they already have with his daughter.

Then one morning as she and Edna (the Baums' other house girl) come to begin their work, Romonah is bitten by a snake! The cobra as lying alongside the doorway, mostly hidden underneath a mat. When she stepped on it, the snake struck her near the ankle. It is six o'clock. Marion and I are just stirring in bed when we hear the high-pitched scream. I bound out of bed, slip into my clothes and run outside without my shoes.

By this time the Baums have gotten up as well and Gordon has killed the snake. Romonah is in severe pain. She, being an excitable person to begin with, is now expressing herself verbally with screams of pain. Her voice reaches far out into the surrounding veld. Gordon and I try to calm her as we carry her to our house. Once there, I inject the anti–snake bite serum into her leg. By this time the poison has circulated quite a bit due to her excited state. Will she live?

The day happens to be Sunday. We are to attend services planned in several churches, which always include a sermon from the missionary. There is no way of notifying them in time that something else has come up. So it is decided that the women, Marion and her sister, Eileen, will stay home to look after Romonah. and the men go on to the churches. I go off in one direction and Gordon with his group another way. I preach at the services and see many come to Christ for salvation. Most of the day is spent on the plains in Mbugwe.

During my absence, Romonah almost leaves us. Marion and Eileen keep on praying fervently for her recovery. They ask the Lord to spare her life, as she is still needed here. She loves the Wambugwe. Even though she is an outsider from Kenya, she has accepted them as her own people and they, in turn, have taken her in as one of them. No one wants her to leave at this time. Marion and Eileen get ahold of the Lord and plead with Him to allow her to stay on with them.

As the day wears on, Romonah drifts off into unconsciousness. Asphyxiation sets in. Her eyes roll back, her mouth dries, and her breathing slows down to a minimum. Water is dripped into her mouth. She is starting to slip away. The two sisters continue to pray. One of them reads the words of Jesus as recorded in Mark 16:17–18; "And these signs shall follow them that believe; in my name shall they cast out devils, they shall speak with new tongues. They shall take up serpents and if they drink any deadly thing it shall not hurt them, they shall lay hands on the sick and they shall recover."

Romonah explains to us later that during this time she can hear the women as in the distance through a long tunnel. Then, instead of drifting further away she starts to return slowly. Drawing nearer to the praying women, she hears them more clearly. Jesus had stayed her ascent and reversed her direction of travel. He tells Romonah that she will not die.

It is at this moment that she opens her eyes and looks at Marion and Eileen beside her. The Lord has truly touched her and healed her! He has allowed her to remain here to keep pouring out her love on those she loves and who love her. The sisters rejoice and praise the One Who has answered their prayers.

When I return, I find to my amazement Romonah sitting up and able to talk. It is a miracle! Marion informs me of how Romonah had almost gone to be with the Lord. Only their prayerful vigil had stayed the hand of the angel of death. Lest she forget the miracle, Romonah is left with a pain where the snake had bitten her, a reminder of her escape from death.

Romonah lives on to marry Eliezer Mdobi, who becomes

one of the national leaders in the church. I will never forget that wedding! By this time I am fairly well acquainted with the Swahili language. But even so, I make a mistake in the pronunciation of one word in their marriage ceremony. Not one of those present corrects me even after I make the same mistake repeatedly. It is only months afterwards that I learn of my blooper!

The people of Africa are gracious and considerate. They do not immediately correct the person who is just learning a language so as not to cause him to feel embarrassed. Because of this practice, Marion and I will never know how many mistakes we did make during our earlier years of learning Swahili. Whenever I would overhear Marion misuse a word while working with the house girls in the kitchen, I would turn on the girls for not correcting her. Their answer was simply: "We know what she really means."

As I said earlier, it is months before I learn of the mistake I made at Romonah and Eliezer's wedding, when Marion and I are part of the audience observing a drama being performed at the closing exercises of Bible School. Africans love drama, in which they excel. Today they are reenacting Romonah and Eliezer's wedding and Romonah is playing the part of the minister (me).

Am I hearing correctly? To peals of hilarious laughter from the audience, Romonah is repeatedly invoking the Lord to "bless this bucket." Yes, there can be no doubt. Just one letter differentiates the words for marriage and bucket. Marriage is *ndoa,* and bucket is *ndoo.* Throughout the solemn marriage ceremony I had fervently petitioned the Lord to "bless this bucket"!

I am glad that the Lord understood what I really meant that day. How do I know? Because God has been blessing their marriage. They have several daughters to prove it.

*   *   *

Before I close this chapter I wish to add another incident where a man survived the bite from a poisonous snake. Many residing in remote areas, of course, do not survive. Before help arrives, they succumb to death. In spite of various kinds of snakes about us at Kaiti, the family and I were never struck by one of them. Many close calls, though. I have shared those incidents in my book *In the Tanganyika Bush,* in chapter 11.

One morning Richard, a worker on the mission station, saunters over to where I am seated on our veranda. He gives the customary greeting: *"Habari, yako?"* ("How are you?") I answer him that I am fine. Then he asks, *"Habari ya nyumbani?"* ("How is it at home?") Again I repeat that all is well. A few more questions—about the welfare of the wife and of the children—are asked before I break in to ask him how he is. He answers quietly, *"Mzuri, lakini nimeumwa na nyoka"* ("Fine, but I have been bitten by a snake").

I can hardly believe it! Whereas Romonah screamed and carried on, Richard stands there calm and unperturbed. The only thing different about him that I notice is his holding his arm by the wrist during the exchange of greetings. He now explains how it all happened. While he was repairing the roof of his hut, when he was inserting the new grass, a cobra hidden from view struck him on the wrist! Could I now help him?

Marion and I call upon the Lord to keep the poison from spreading any farther. Richard's current lethargic state is to his advantage. I lance the openings where the fangs have punctured his wrist and suck out what I can of the poison within the wound. I have done what I could. We have no anti–snake bite serum on hand. The Lord must do the rest if Richard is to live.

Two hours later, when Marion and I are preparing to leave for a service with the Masai, Richard is ready to accompany us! He tells us that he feels fine. There are no noticeable aftereffects. All he has to show for his ordeal with a poisonous snake, besides the fang marks on his wrist, is a lump in his armpit. The poison had stopped there on its way to the heart. The Lord had caught it in time! Hallelujah!

Chapter Four

A Regrettable Incident

Marion and I are ready to leave for Kaiti. We have been here in Uburunge for the weekend holding services at various meeting points. Several students from the Bible school came with us to assist us in our efforts to plant churches in this tribe. As usual, we have come with the red pickup. It is now time to return home.

We bid farewell to the congregation at Goima and then pull away slowly in our GMC. Before I can get very far, a girl in her teens from a nearby hut crawls onto the back where our passengers are seated. I stop and walk around to enquire what she is doing there?

She answers in Swahili, "I am coming along with you to Kaiti."

"To do what?" I ask her.

"To live at the mission and hear more about Christ and His ways. Also, to learn about cooking and housekeeping as others have," is her reply.

I am reluctant to take her along, especially when I learn that she did not get permission from her elderly father. She admits that she is running away from home. Her name is Zilipa. We often have runaway girls come to the mission, wishing either to attend the Bible classes we prepare for the youth or just to stay and work for the missionaries. So Zilipa is not the first one. But in her case now I would be assisting her, while with the ones in Mbugwe the girls just showed up one day at our door. We cannot chase them away, even when their fathers show up to retrieve them. We always leave it up to the runaway girl to decide her own future.

Angelina, who is currently working for Marion in the house, was one of those runaway girls. She had accepted Christ at one of our churches in Mbugwe and, when she found it hard to keep her faith in a pagan home, fled to the mission. There she was enrolled in the Bible classes for the youth. The father tried several times to draw her away but to no avail. Had she stepped off the compound to converse with him, he would have seized her and then dragged her home. We then would have been unable to interfere. But Angelina makes sure that she remains in the haven of the mission.

Angelina is determined to remain at the mission, and we employ her. She then enrolls in our Bible school along with another girl from Mbugwe, Francine. Both do very well in their studies, much to the chagrin of the male student body. When it comes to preaching, both girls surpass most of them. Her father and mother, along with her sisters, all accept the Lord eventually. Angelina is an asset to the work of God and assists Marion and me in our evangelistic trips to Uburunge. She is there when Zilipa climbs onto the back of our pickup in an endeavour to join those already at Kaiti Mission.

As I mentioned previously, I am hesitant to allow Zilipa to remain on the vehicle because her father would see it as me running away with his daughter, no matter that I have a wife, as polygamy is common here in Uburunge. I order Zilipa to step down from the back of the pickup. She refuses. I repeat, "You must come down. You cannot go along. Maybe next time, after you have been granted permission from your father."

Zilipa unwillingly climbs down. Her attempt to escape has failed, and it is my fault. She does not look at me and I quickly get behind the wheel before I change my mind. But it is not over yet. Before I can shift into second, Zilipa has hopped back into the pickup! I stop and walk over to reprimand her. She is quiet during the whole monologue. Nothing is going to dislodge her this time. So I give in and return to see if I can get permission from her father to take Zilipa along.

Lee (pronounced "lay") is a well-known witch doctor in the area and is much feared for his strong medicines. He is up in years, at least eighty-five, and has several wives. His last one is the mother of Zilipa. Both mother and daughter have accepted Christ, but Lee has kept himself aloof. He wishes to die and go to where his ancestors have gone. He is not interested in any other way or place.

It does not take long to acquire the permission for Zilipa to travel with us to Kaiti. Her mother readily agrees and after a short discourse with the old witch doctor, he gives his approval as well. I suppose he is looking ahead to when Zilipa will be worth more dowry to him as it comes time to marry her off. Girls who are educated always fetch more cows or hard cash! Yes, let her go and learn the ways of the white people.

At this moment there is no one more thrilled than Zilipa. She is beaming with happiness!

As with all runaway girls, she comes with no suitcase or bundle. All that she possesses is what she is wearing. When we arrive at the mission her hair is sprayed to get rid of any lice she may have, a regular routine that new girls go through before taking up residence at the station. Zilipa then proceeds to attend the classes in progress for the youth. In spite of not knowing how to read, she does quite well.

It is not long before she is hired on as one of our house girls. Zilipa learns quickly under the supervision of Marion and the watchful eye of Angelina, our now more experienced worker in the house. Earlier Angelina herself had apprenticed under Elizabeth (Chembe), who previously had learned from Florence, our first house girl, whom we had brought down from Kenya. Marion therefore always had someone with her who assisted in the training of the new girl in the house.

On our monthly treks to Uburunge, Zilipa comes along with us to visit her friends. When we are about to leave, she is always ready to return with Marion and me to Kaiti. She does not want to remain home. Then, when the father begins talking about marrying her off, she refuses to accompany us on most of our journeys to Uburunge. She is afraid that he may force her at any time to stay home.

Because Marion and I are planning this time to stay on in Uburunge for two weeks, Zilipa and Angelina accompany us. During this time we learn that Lee is negotiating the dowry of Zilipa with someone. We drive over to visit Lee. No amount of talking deters him from his plan of marrying off his daughter to the man. It does not matter that she does not like the man. It does not matter that he already has a wife. What matters is that Lee himself is getting older and wants the dowry before he dies. Still, I continue to refuse the marriage on behalf of Zilipa.

One day a messenger arrives on foot at our safari house at Aimabu, where we are staying while here in Uburunge. The message is that I, along with Zilipa, am to appear the following day at the courthouse in Goima. The old witch doctor has taken his case to the local authorities. Naturally, they will be sympathetic to their tribal customs. So what chance do we have? To say that Zilipa cannot marry the man as he already has a wife will not win the case in the polygamist tribe. The man who wants Zilipa is a teacher at Goima and hails from a faraway tribe near Lake Victoria. He has the money ready for her dowry.

Early in the morning Zilipa and I arrive at the *baraza* (courthouse), which is nothing more than an empty building except for a table and chair inside it. There the official is seated while those attending the hearing are squatted on the floor along the wall on both sides. The front end of the building has no wall or door but is open all the way across. Anyone outside is able to see and hear the proceedings of any case should he or she be curious enough. And they are! There is always time for that.

There is a short wait while a few minor cases are being taken care of, and then Zilipa and I are ushered into the *baraza*. The old witch doctor states his case, that the daughter refuses to consent his arrangement of her marriage. Zilipa is then questioned as to why she is refusing. She tells the official that she does not like the man. That goes over like a lead balloon! What has that got to do with the whole affair anyway? The man she is to marry is wealthy and will take care of her, the court reasons. Zilipa again states that she will not be the man's wife. The old man repeats that she must marry the man.

When I am asked what I have to say about the case, I reply that as long as Zilipa refuses I will stand by her. "Besides," I add "the man has a wife, and in our Christian belief the gospel does not allow for someone to take a second wife in marriage. Polygamy is contrary to our teachings."

The court listens and respects what I have just said. It is now up to the old man to drop the case. He replies that he will if I, in return, will pay the dowry. It is obvious that he is after the bride price for Zilipa. No matter who pays for it! I know enough that if I do pay it, then she will be considered my wife according to their tribal custom.

Here now is a quick solution to her case. But there is no way I can agree to it. What to do? I request that the case be adjourned so that I have some days to think about it. I must stall for time, hoping that in the meantime something else will develop. Maybe the man who wants to marry Zilipa has now seen that she does not want him. Surely he must have been embarrassed by her confession in front of the whole courtroom! But he is not.

Marion and I, along with Zilipa, manage to make our exodus from Uburunge without a further incident. Lee still wants the dowry. He will not wait long. And he does not. Negotiations with the teacher are resumed, and Lee accepts the first down payment. It is now up to the old man to present his daughter to the teacher.

When we next appear in Uburunge, Zilipa is told by her mother that the father is going to perform witchcraft in order to bring her back home. This piece of news startles Zilipa. All the way back to Kaiti, she sits speechless. Marion and I talk to her about it. She is not to be afraid so long as she believes in the protection of Jesus Christ, who is stronger than any witch doctor.

She remains troubled. "You do not know my father. He is a very strong witch doctor," she tells us. "I have seen him use his magic and it works!" Zilipa adds. Then she goes on to relate how her brother had run away to Mwanza, where he stayed for some time. When he failed to return, the father performed his witchcraft and the boy, hundreds of miles away, was suddenly struck with homesickness. It affected him so much that he returned home in spite of his not wanting to do so!

With prayer and some counselling, Zilipa's spirit is lifted from under the cloud of despondency. She returns to her old self. But, two days later, Angelina rushes in to inform us that Zilipa is talking of going home! What? We talk to her and it is so. Yes, she wishes to return home.

"Do you know that this now means your father will give you to the teacher?" I ask. "Do you love him?"

To this she answers, "No!"

Marion and I counsel her and pray with her again. Soon she snaps out of it and declares forcibly that she does not wish to return home.

The power of witchcraft is strong. It was reaching across from Goima, 135 miles away, and tugging at Zilipa to return to the one performing it. When under the spell, she is like in a trance. She wants only one thing, and that is to go home. And when the power of God breaks the spell she is free of this longing. When reminded of her actions, she shudders to think that she had actually wanted to go back to Goima.

Zilipa has another spell two days later. Angelina finds her packing her box to leave for home. Marion and I, with God's help, retrieve her again from the spell of witchcraft that her father has put upon her. But we notice that it takes longer this time for her to recover. We are with her more, and she carries on normally. Maybe she will be alright now. Surely the old man will give up. Satan must have seen by now that he is defeated.

It is Saturday and we need to go to Arusha for some supplies. Marion and I leave very early so that we can be back by dark. It is a seventy-five-mile drive to town, but it takes all of two hours to travel the distance. When we return to the mission at dusk, Angelina greets us with the news that Zilipa is gone! She left soon after our departure. Where she previously had forewarned Angelina by saying that she wished to go or packing her box, this time Zilipa said nothing and left without a thing. Before Angelina knew what was happening, she was on her way to the road to catch a vehicle for Kondoa and then Goima.

I drive quickly to check at Mdori. Maybe Zilipa has failed to procure a vehicle. But I am informed that she did board a bus for Kondoa in the forenoon. She is gone! Why did we not take the girls along? Had we done that, she would still be here. It is too late to follow her to Goima. I pray that she may yet come to her senses in time. Or is it too late already?

The following day, Marion and I are scheduled to attend one of the churches in Mbugwe where I am to bring the message. This prevents us from going to Uburunge to check on Zilipa. But we decide to go there on Monday for sure. When we return home in the evening we find one of Zilipa's brothers waiting for us. He has come for her clothes and the rest of her belongings. Yes, she arrived yesterday afternoon. She walked the ten miles from the Great North Road. And, yes, she now is married!

We do not go to Uburunge on Monday. It no longer is necessary. But we do go a week later. Arriving in Goima, we spot Zilipa the same time she sees us. She comes running to us and falls into Marion's lap before we are able to step out of the vehicle. She sobs and apologizes for what she had done, repeating that she did not know what she was doing until it was too late. Upon her arrival she had found her father waiting. It is then that I recall Zilipa's mother saying how the father had predicted that she would be home within a week. His words came true!

Zilipa goes on to say that the very same evening she was carried to the home of the teacher, who was expecting her. The custom in Uburunge concerning a girl who is betrothed to be married is that she must be carried from her home to the groom's place on the shoulders of young men of the clan. I personally have seen this on several occasions where fellows were running across the fields with a maiden on their backs. Usually the girl is clad in a white cloth. She, of course, is screaming and crying, announcing to all that she is being kidnapped. Often it is staged, to show her girlfriends that she has been chosen from among them. But in Zilipa's case, the protests were real as they carted her away.

No man can turn back the clock. If one could, then I would have done it that day. But now this continues to remain a regrettable memory of an incident that I wish I could relive and change.

Chapter Five

Nighttime Adventures

It is around midnight when Marion is awakened from a deep sleep by a *"Hodi?"* ("May I come in?") by someone outside the window. I am away at this time visiting the work in Uburunge, and Marion had decided to stay behind with Mark, Colleen and Kirk being away at boarding school. She now asks the man outside what the problem is. He answers that Leba, one of the deacons at the Milima Mitatu church, is very ill. Can she come to help him?

The man at her window is a stranger, but she feels that he is telling her the truth. She decides to go and check on his condition in spite of the late hour. Leba is one of the first men in Mbugwe to accept Christ and is still in the church. It is not right to forsake him now in his hour of need. The stranger outside does not go into detail on what it is that Leba is suffering from.

Marion dresses and locks the door behind her as she leaves the house. She trusts that Mark will be safe during her absence. When she is about to enter the red pickup, she remembers that the battery had been removed earlier. While she is replacing it, she is thinking, *Will I know how to connect it properly? Lord, help me to know which cable goes where.* With that prayer on her lips, she clips on the cables. When she gets inside the cab and turns the key, the engine starts right off. "Thank you, Lord!" she exclaims.

The stranger crawls onto the back of the pickup, and Marion drives over to awaken Eliezer, the pastor, and John, the dispenser. They are to accompany her on this night drive. After questioning the man from Milima Mitatu a bit more, the two move to one side and talk something over in a low tone. Then they return to their homes and each one comes back out with a weapon in his hand, one with a spear and the other with a *panga* (machete). They are not about to venture off into the night without some protection.

There is no incident along the two-mile drive in the dark, and they reach the deacon's house shortly. At least 100 people are gathered around the hut. In Africa the night does not hold back news from travelling. Marion shines her torch (flashlight) around as she walks to the hut. They blend so well into the darkness. Their blankets are wrapped around themselves, covering even their faces, except for the eyes. There is only a slight chill in the air.

Entering the hut, she discovers it full of Wambugwe. She asks many of them to leave in order to allow some air to flow in from the outside. It is dark, the only light of any kind coming from the amber of live coals in a fireplace where food was cooked earlier over three stones. Marion has to rely on her torch to see properly. She locates Leba on the floor. He is going through spasms, and six men are pinning him down. His eyes are wide open, with a wild yet pleading look in them, and he has lost his speech.

Marion is told that Leba was fine until suppertime. Shortly after eating his evening meal, he started having convulsions. The spasms that contract his whole body are so severe that he now is entirely exhausted. She then hears someone whisper the word, "Poison"! If Leba has been poisoned, what should now be done? This tribe so steeped in witchcraft uses poison to rid themselves of unwanted individuals. This is possibly the case right now.

There has been only one previous experience, Marion remembers, where I came upon someone who had been poisoned. This was soon after our arrival in Tanganyika. I had just finished a service at Magara when word came to me from the village across the river that a child was dying. Could I help them? I rushed over and found the hut crowded with mourners. The child, a girl about six years old, was unconscious on the dirt floor.

I discovered that her jaws were locked. I also noticed that the medicine man had been forcing his concoction into her mouth through the opening in her teeth. (The two lower teeth in front of most tribal members are removed during childhood for purposes such as this one.) There was also some of his *dawa* (medicine) in her ears. I explained to them that the only way I could help them was with prayer. God could heal the child, I told them. I laid my hands on the young girl and prayed for her healing.

I questioned them as to what had happened to the child, but no one was anxious to assist me. I then searched the girl's limbs for any open wounds that could be infected. There were none, so it could not be tetanus. No sign of a snake bite either. The only other thing it could be was poisoning, I thought. I then ordered that someone fetch me milk quickly. As soon as it arrived, I poured some of it down her throat through the *pengo* (gap between teeth).

I kept forcing milk into the girl's mouth until finally she began vomiting it back up. The jaws unlocked and she sat up. The father and mother began to thank me and promised not to allow the medicine man to apply any more of his *dawa* on the child. The Lord had undertaken for her welfare. She was smiling at me before I left their home. The next time we entered their village she was back to normal. Before we left, we conducted a service, and the girl with her father were the first ones to accept Christ. A church was planted.

Marion now calls for milk to be brought to her. If it worked for me, it should here as well. When it arrives she gets them to mix some salt into it. Then it is given to Leba little by little until the mixture is all down in his stomach. It does not take long and he begins to expel the contents. More milk with salt mixed into it is given him. He again retches and vomits up the mixture along with the poison.

She collects a sample of what he has discharged into a gourd so as to take it to Arusha and have it analyzed by a lab technician. Marion continues to pray for the man's complete healing. His wife has been sitting during this whole time in the corner, frightened and not saying anything. The deacon begins to calm down and commences to say a few words. Marion mentions then to him that she ought to be going. There is fear in his eyes now, so she asks several of the Christians to stay with him the rest of the night.

When Marion and her two companions from the mission are leaving the scene, she realizes that she has forgotten the specimen of the poison in the hut. As she reverses the pickup, the taillight does not reveal the stump that blends in with the black night and she hits it. All three heads inside the cab snap back and smack into the rear window, shattering it. Telltale cracks reveal that there were three heads that smashed into the glass.

By this time the whole episode is getting to Marion: the eeriness of the night, the whispers in the crowd, the screaming of the deacon, the possibility of the wife trying to do away with her husband, and now the breaking of the window on our imported vehicle! *Will we be able to purchase another window here, or do we have to order it from Canada?* she asks herself.

They arrive back at the mission as the cock begins to crow. She retires to the bedroom, but no sleep comes to her. Fear grips her, and she seeks the Lord for help, knowing that He is the only one who can remove it. She kneels beside the bed and prays until the fear leaves her.

In the morning after breakfast Marion returns to visit her patient. Leba is weak but much better. She has them give him more milk to drink and then prays for him. The wife is no longer there, but his children are present to care for him. She bids them farewell and leaves.

When I return home from my safari to Uburunge, Marion informs me of what transpired during my absence. The following day we take the specimen to Arusha to be tested at the lab and Marion is told that the milk has already neutralized the poison. There is now no way to know what kind of poison it was that the wife used. The woman is shunned by her friends, and from that day on she begins to walk alone. She is now branded as a witch. Whenever Marion entertains women on our veranda and she appears, they all quit eating.

* * *

Late one night, Marion and I are awakened by a "*Hodi?*" at our bedroom window, which is always ajar due to the hot weather. It is someone asking for help to take his wife to the small maternity hospital at Magugu, twenty miles south of here. She is hemorrhaging and needs immediate care. I decide to go and tell Marion that it should not take me more than an hour and a half to make the trip. She replies that she will wait up for me.

I drive up to the hut at Nchemu and discover that the woman has just given birth to a stillborn baby. She is bleeding profusely and will surely die if she does not get to a doctor soon. We load her into the vehicle, and with her husband along, I head back to the main road and before long I am at the maternity wing of the hospital. It takes a while to find someone, as they are all asleep. Finally, someone who looks like a doctor comes over to look at the patient.

He takes a quick look at the woman, without removing her from my vehicle, and informs me that she needs a blood transfusion, for there has been a lot of blood lost already. Then he adds that they are unable to perform it here, as they lack the equipment and facility for it. I should take her to Arusha.

Now, I had not expected this! That is ninety-five miles away. Will I make it in time? No use wasting any more of it. I turn the vehicle back onto the Great North Road and head north. When I see the mission sign in the headlights, I do not turn in to brief Marion of my necessity to take the bleeding woman on to the hospital in Arusha. I dare not take the time.

Except for a few animals on the road, I meet no traffic as I speed through the night. Finally, I deliver the woman safely to the hospital, and before long she is admitted for an examination. Yes, she will need to have a blood transfusion immediately and lots of it. They check the husband's blood and discover it is not of the right type. Someone with the right blood to match hers will have to be found quickly if she is to live.

The nurse asks me for my blood type. It is the same as the sick woman's. "Will you be willing to donate your blood?" the nurse asks me. How can I refuse? Before long I see my blood flowing into a container that will save the life of the woman I brought with me from Mbugwe. After it is over, the nurse tells me to take it easy for an hour. But I cannot. I must get back home, as Marion will be wondering by now why I am taking so long.

It is five in the morning when I pull into the yard. The house girl greets me at the door and explains that the Mama has gone searching for me. They had been called in to watch Mark until her return. Oh, no! Now why did she do that? I crawl back inside the vehicle and drive out to the spot on the

40

main road where I turned off to take the trail to Nchemu. Here I stop and get out to check the tracks. I find mine turning off and then back on to go south to Magugu. There are no other tracks on top of mine. Marion has gone on to Magugu.

It does not take me long to decide what to do next. I am not about to travel to Magugu for the second time in one night! Too tired for that, I return home and lie down for some shut-eye. Marion will discover that I had to go to Arusha from the doctor at Magugu and come on back home. Just as I drift off to sleep there is a banging at the front door. It is Marion. I had absentmindedly locked it.

The sun is now peeking over the Tarangire forest. No one is going to bed anymore. Marion now shares her side of the story. After I left with the man, she had read for two hours. Then, when I still had not returned after another hour, she began to think something had happened to me. So she called the girls in to watch Mark and made plans to search for me. She got Eliezer and Richard, our gardener, to go along with her.

She drove straight on to the hospital at Magugu where I was to have taken the woman. After hunting around in the dark for someone on the medical staff, they found him sleeping. When Marion asked him whether I had been there, he answered her that no white man had come that night. *So where can he be?* she wondered. They returned to the vehicle and made their way back to Kaiti.

Travelling along they used the torches they had brought along. The ditches were checked to make sure I was not there. When they found no sign of me, she decided to go the village where I was to pick up the lady. When they reached the right hut, they had to wake up its occupants, as it was now five o'clock. Marion learned that I had been there and taken the woman, with her husband, on to the hospital from where she had just come, in Magugu. Now she was really puzzled.

41

She drove back to the main road and stopped there to examine the tracks. But she was unable to tell where mine led. Not knowing what else to do, she decided to return home. When she drove into the yard, much to her amazement, she discovered my car. And when she tried the door, it was locked. She called my name several times, but no answer. Only when she banged on the door did I wake up.

A week later the woman returns to Mbugwe from Arusha. She has fully recovered. And no, she has not turned into an *Mzungu* (white person) in spite of the blood from one flowing in her veins. Ever since word had gotten around that the missionary had donated his blood to her, many had been saying that she would now turn into an *Mzungu*. But she is an African and will always be one.

Chapter Six

Thefts

Throughout our years at Kaiti we do not employ a watchman on the mission compound. We are far enough away from town that we do not attract the common run of thieves. The Wambugwe and Masai know us as their friends and respect us and our property. As well, I believe, the wild carnivora of the night play a large role in keeping troublemakers near their homes. The lion, leopard, and hyena act as watchdogs! One would put his own life in danger by wandering around after dark.

There are two separate incidents where we do get robbed. Oh yes, there are several other minor thefts, such as the children "losing" some of their toys. After they played with the items, one would be overlooked and left outside in the sand. Or at times it may be a knife or a spoon that is forgotten out on the veranda. They usually are found the next day in the yard boy's possession. He had seen them lying outside and taken them to his home. When confronted and asked why he had stolen them, he simply replies that he thought we did not want them any more and had thrown them away.

They count themselves most fortunate to come upon things lying around unattended. Even a blessing from God! I still remember the day a young mother who walks twenty miles in order to visit us came across a pair of sandals lying beside the road. She was still rejoicing over her find when she arrived to tell us how the Lord had blessed her with a pair of shoes. I wonder what the owner of those sandals thought when she discovered them gone. The old saying "finders keepers, losers weepers" is often applicable out here. Stealing is only when you catch the person in the act and can prove that the item is yours.

While we are away for a week, someone comes and breaks the padlock on the storeroom. He steals some flour, used clothing (which we have just received from Canada), and nails. Then he is off, the loot hidden inside a bag slung over his shoulder. It is night.

As we pull into the yard, we discover our workers standing around waiting for us. They immediately inform us that there has been a robbery. Upon inspection, I conclude that the thief must be a strong man. With a bar he easily twisted off the padlock on the metal door. But he is an amateur! It had rained some, and he came soon afterwards. His tracks are there for all to see. They reveal that he has one big toe missing!

We all know right away who the thief is. He is someone who worked for the mission a while back, a big man with one of his big toes missing. They call him Tembo Saba (Seven Elephants) because of his size and strength. What helps us even more in our tracking him right to his place is that he has a hole in the pocket of his shorts he is wearing. A nail drops out every now and then.

It does not take us long to cover the two miles to his hut. The goods are recovered. Tembo Saba admits he stole them because he was hungry and needed clothes. But why the nails? "To fix my roof" is the answer. I forgive him and do not report the incident to the chief. But Michael hears about it anyway and is not pleased that I allowed Tembo Saba to go unpunished. I guess Christian love and forgiveness are difficult to comprehend.

*   *   *

Driving into our yard after a Sunday service, we hear Mickey, our Pekingese, barking excitedly behind the house where the Baums are living. It seems a bit strange for him to be making such a fuss at this time of the day, since it is only about two o'clock. He usually carries on at dusk, when the leopard is roaming about somewhere in the tall grass or in the nearby riverbed. If it were not for Mickey, we would never know that the spotted cat is out there. The leopard is a master at concealing himself; only his rasping cough, given at regular intervals, gives away his position.

Marion and I approach the door to our kitchen and immediately notice that the mosquito screen is torn and the window that opens into our dining room ajar! I enter quickly and discover the back door wide open. Going outside to check further, I find Mickey still barking and looking off into the bush behind the Baums' house.

After a quick examination inside, we find several items missing. Nothing large, just soap, shoe polish, and the like. When Gordon and Eileen pull in they discover that their house has been broken into as well! The thief had entered by prying open one of the doors. Here he stole several items as well, one of them being Gordon's hunting knife. The offering money from the churches in Mbugwe for the past month is missing, too. Again, nothing large was removed.

We conclude that the thief is alone and on foot. Marion and I had interrupted his search for more things to steal. This explains why only a few items are missing from our house. When we drove in he fled out the back way. It was easy for him to open the door, as the key was in the lock, which he took with him, unfortunately.

I climb up the big sausage tree behind Baums' house and stare across the tall grass and bushes in the direction where the dog had been barking. Maybe I may still catch a glimpse of the thief making his way to safety. I do not spot him anywhere. Next, Gordon and I decide to drive out to the open flats just beyond all this wilderness. We may run across him out there.

But there is no suspicious-looking character carrying a bag of loot. We enquire at a small shop, the only one out here on the Mbugwe flats, and they inform us that no one has come to spend or change coins into notes. The church offering was in coins. I did not think the thief would want to go very far with a sack full of them.

Next, we decide to drive to the nearest police station, which is at Babati, thirty-five miles away, to report the theft. We head out to the Great North Road and turn south. Just beyond the pyramidal hills, we see a stranger ahead flagging us down for a lift. And he is holding a white sack in his hands! Can this be our man? What luck if it is!

Gordon slows down and stops the Fiat. I ask the man outside, "Where are you wishing to go?"

He answers, "Babati."

That is where we are going, too. "Hop in," I tell him. I look back at him as he is entering the station wagon and am convinced that this is the thief. The white bag he is clutching is one of our pillow cases!

I reach back to peek inside the bag, and sure enough, I recognize the contents. "This is the thief!" I exclaim to Gordon. The man immediately backs out the door, which he had not yet closed behind him. I had been too hasty in my declaration, not realizing that he might know English. I should have waited until he was seated and we were on our way to the police station.

The thief takes off running, leaving the bag of loot in my hand. I crawl out and bolt after him. He strikes out across the cultivated fields with me a few strides behind him. As I begin to gain on him, he pulls out of his pockets the stolen coins and tosses them on the ground. "Here they are; now leave me!" he shouts. I take a quick look around and notice we are near a termite mound. Must remember this and stay on his heels.

When he has emptied his pockets and I still stay on his back, he turns suddenly and brandishes the stolen hunting knife in my face. He is desperate. We stare at each other. The distance between us is only twelve feet—that is, four paces. I bend down quickly and scoop up a rock the size of my fist and threaten to throw it at him. He turns and runs. The chase is on! I bound after him, the stone still in my hand.

After a mile of flat-out running, the thief starts to draw away from me. He has more going for him; the fear of imprisonment. Just as I am beginning to think that he may make good his escape, Gordon pulls up with the vehicle. He found a place to cross over the fields and has caught up to me in time. I hop in beside Gordon and we light out after the running thief with the Fiat. The man now has no chance of getting away.

But the thief is not about to give up so easily. He dodges first this way and then that way whenever the vehicle is about to knock him down. But he cannot keep this up. Soon he is exhausted and comes to a standstill. I leap out and charge him. The thief raises his arm, and believing that he is about to strike me with the knife, I grab his arm and fling him over my shoulder, slamming him to the ground. I do not let go but quickly twist the arm behind his back as he lies facedown in the dust. It is now I notice that there is no knife in his hand. I ask him, "Where is the knife?"

"What knife?" he replies. Then he starts to deny the charge of theft and claims he knows nothing of what we are talking about. He even accuses me of wrongly chasing him and then manhandling him as I did. We ignore his babble and tie him up hand and foot with a rope that Gordon finds inside his vehicle.

We drive back in our tracks and come to the spot where I was picked up by Gordon. There is a fallen tree nearby. I feel impressed to have a look around. A good thing we stopped. I discover the knife lying right next to the fallen tree. The thief tossed it there when we were not looking. This evidence should now convict him.

As we near the main road, we stop at the termite mound and retrieve the coins that the thief dropped during his flight. We recover most of the money that was stolen. Reaching the road, we head for Babati to report the theft and turn in the thief. Upon arrival at the police station, the man is locked in a cell. When asked for his identity card, he replies that he does not have one. He is told to strip, and they search his clothing. Nothing. Who is the man anyway? Where does he come from?

Gordon goes outside and searches his vehicle. Maybe the man dropped his ID card there. And it is so. While lying in the back of the station wagon all tied up, he was still able to fish out his ID card and slip it behind the seat. The card reveals that he is a Kenyan. The police ask him what he is doing out here, so far from home. His answer does not satisfy the police. It is obvious that he is on the run, stealing whatever he can find to carry with him.

The police ask us to return in a week's time for the hearing. Until then the stolen items must remain with them as evidence. So we leave the pillowcase with its contents, except for the money, behind and return to Kaiti. I feel uneasy about surrendering the key to our back door. A copy can easily be made of it by one of them, and they gain entrance to our home when we are not around. Must change the lock on it.

When Gordon and I arrive at the mission, we find it crowded with Christians from the church. Has the news of the robbery gotten around so quickly? Marion and Eileen report that they have been awaiting the results of our trip. We inform everyone of what had taken place, of our chase and eventually catching the thief. They rejoice and give thanks to God for returning the offering that had been stolen. "You cannot steal from God and get away with it!" they cheer.

As we had been ordered, Gordon and I return to the police in Babati for the hearing and to reclaim the articles that had been stolen. To our surprise we learn that the thief has escaped. Two days ago, when the one who feeds the prisoners was setting out their evening meal, our thief just walks off and disappears into the shadows! The cook was not about to chase after him and leave the other prisoners unattended. Where were the police officers? Oh, they were quenching their thirst at the nearby bar.

There is nothing more we can do. All our things have been recovered. These we now pick up from the police, and we head on back home. The case is now officially closed.

There are similarities between the two incidents of theft we experienced at Kaiti. Both times the thieves were caught and both times they escaped being punished. The only difference is that I agreed to the first one.

Tembo Saba and Chembe (Elizabeth).

Cooking on three stones.

Marion and Kirk with the old lady at Aimabu.

Baking biscuits on live coals outside.

Hatari with John Wayne, filmed in Arusha.

In our backyard with Colleen's dog, Mickey.

An Mburunge grinding millet on her stone.

Stirring her *ugali* while it is cooking.

Running off the *Mpanzi* on the duplicator.

Elizabeth bathing Mark and Kirk.

Colleen and Alex Baum, part of Romonah and Eliezer's wedding.

James Chimbalambala names his twins: Marion and Stanley.

Elizabeth, Angelina, Zilipa, and Marion.

The bushbuck that the Lord brought to our door.

One of many ulcers needing treatment.

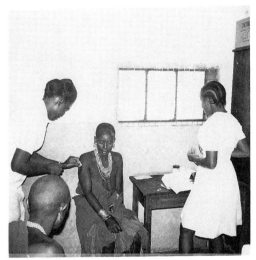

The sick being treated in our dispensary.

Colleen with little Colleen Mdobi.

An Mbugwe named both of her girls after Marion.

What's Mark up to next?

Kirk and Colleen looking down on Mirambo Mission.

Bible school for youth during vacation time.

Francine, one of our women pastors.

Njela and Tenu in front of the house built for them by the mission.

Waiting for water to seep in at a dry riverbed in Uburunge.

Lee accepts Christ before we leave Tanzania.

The tabernacle gets completed in time for our farewell.

Chapter Seven

He Will Provide

Marion and I came out by faith to Africa. We did not come with the backing of a missionary board or of a church. We knew if we were to survive out there in the mission field, it would have to be by trusting entirely on the Lord for His assistance. And for nine years it was so. This does not mean that we now do not live by faith since joining the missionary board, as we still must pray for the funds to carry on our various programs. But our immediate needs are looked after by the missionary board at the current time.

When we left Canada for Africa, there had been no time to travel the field so as to raise funds or procure pledges of support. Because of the way we were leaving, independent of the missionary board, most churches and individuals we knew were not about to invest in a couple who are leaving home and going to, of all places, dark Africa. The norm is always that you are sent. But here was a couple who said they were called!

Right from the beginning we learned to trust the Lord for our every need. We had to if we were to survive! The result was that He always came through, whether it was for our physical needs or for the material needs of the work. Never in abundance, but always enough. It was amazing how He provided supporters from various parts of the United States and Canada. Many of them we had never met before!

During our years as faith missionaries, we were very

conservative with spending donations for our personal needs. Rather, we wished to put as much as possible into the new work. We did not want the donors to think that we were misusing their offerings. Consequently, this sacrificial style of living kept us below par physically. But we survived those years, and I believe God blessed us for it.

Because we did not know what life would really be like and where in Africa we would be, we had no knowledge of what to take along for our first five-year term. The few items of clothing we did bring along with us to the field soon faded under the bright Tanganyika sun and wore through from the repeated washings done by hand. But the Lord provides. The children began receiving clothes for their birthdays and Christmases from relatives and friends back in Canada. And when the bundles of used clothing began to arrive, the children searched through them eagerly for anything that might fit them. They were as excited over these clothes as if they were brand-new. Marion and I often discovered something that fit us.

"Freely you have received, freely give" is readily practiced by Marion when she gives her dresses away to those who drop in and have need of them more than she. How often I have noticed her dresses on women walking across the Mbugwe flats. And there are times, when on my way home, that I believe it is Marion and wonder what she is doing out on the dusty plains—on foot! But as I draw nearer, I realize it is not her. She has given away another one of her dresses to someone in need.

There were miracles after miracles of how the Lord supplied the amounts needed for purchasing vehicles and building churches, a Bible school, and a dormitory. Even funds for a tabernacle! There was the Baums' house and then ours. In fact, Kaiti Mission was built with money from donors who had become our partners. This was all made possible by sharing it with the Lord in prayer, then believing that He will transmit our burden for that specific need to someone who was able to help us. To rely on our newsletters alone was not enough. We still needed His assistance.

*   *   *

Not only did the Lord show us that He can provide financially for major requirements, but also perform miracles for lesser needs. Many were the times that food for the table came from unexpected sources. The Wambugwe are a poor people barely able to eke out a living. Yet when the women came to visit Marion, they always brought a gift for her. It could be a bottle of milk, several eggs, some millet, maize on the cob, wild cucumbers, a chicken, or even a goat.

Tenu and Njela are two elderly women we met when we started the church at Kaiti Village. We assist them to the services, as they both are handicapped. Tenu is blind, while Njela is crippled and cannot walk. To get around, Tenu hangs onto the stick that a girl, or someone else, leads her with. They live together, as no one wants to bother with them. So the mission begins to assist them in their livelihood. A permanent structure is erected with funds designated for it from a donor in the United States. We move the two women from their flimsy hut into it.

Tenu and Njela try to assist themselves as much as possible without having to rely entirely on the mission for survival. Someone will lead blind Tenu to the palm forest a mile away, where she cuts down the long slender leaves of the palmetto, which is a young palm tree. She carries them back on her head to crippled Njela, who then splits the palm leaves into strips. Once that is done, she weaves baskets and brooms from them. These they then will try to sell. We buy any that are not sold.

There are times when Tenu with her guide drop in to

chat with Marion over a cup of tea. Then, there are times Marion visits the two women in their home. The house is bare except for three stones in the corner where they cook their *ugali* (maize flour) in a pot that rests on them. There are dry cowskins on the floor that serve as their beds. A couple of three-legged stools complete the arrangement.

The two women have been losing their hens to the genet, a spotted wild cat that thirsts for the blood of chickens. Finally, there is only one chicken left. They hide it under their cooking pot each night so that it will not disappear as well. Then one day, on one of her visits, Tenu carries it to the mission and hands it to Marion as a gift. She gives away her last chicken!

*   *   *

Many are the times we have company dropping in on us unexpectedly. Then, there are those times we are notified ahead of time. This is now one of those times. A runner from Arusha appears with the message that our missionary friends are coming to visit us the following day. They are bringing along some Americans to show them a real mission station in the bush. The message concludes with the hope that it is alright with us.

It is alright, for we love company. As we live out in the bush, visitors are scarce and far between. But this time we are out of meat. Hunting season has closed and so it is not possible to drive out and bring back an animal. This I heave done often in the past when company was coming. To run a deep freeze one needs electricity all day and all night, which we do not have out here. Our diesel generator runs only from seven to about ten every night. No, there is no way of storing meat.

Now, if it would be just our missionary friends who were coming, we would serve them whatever we have on hand and know that they would understand. But now, the American guests who are accompanying them are used to beefsteaks. Some wild meat would have been a really good substitute, especially that of an eland, which makes excellent steak.

What can we do at such short notice? We send someone to Mdori, a mile away on the Great North Road, where often beef is being sold. Mind you, it could be meat from a cow that just died suddenly. Very seldom are cows butchered, as they are a sign of wealth, especially with the tribes around here. Only when they die are they butchered and the meat eaten. We do not buy cow meat if we can help it for this very reason. Also, the beef is most always tough, not tender, like game meat.

The man returns from Mdori with the news that there is no meat for sale. Just as good. Saves us the pains of having to make the decision of whether to buy it or not. Marion is beginning to feel concerned about what she will serve the visitors tomorrow. I suggest that she could bake beans, as that is always a good substitute for meat. I have done this during Bible school, passing out beans now and then to the students instead of meat. (After a hunt they dried the meat, so there was usually some around.)

We have a lot of game available, and it is easily acquired. Hunting season used to be the year around. But recently the laws were changed, and one can now only hunt from July to December. And this is March. We have had to learn to do without wild meat and eat more chicken, or beans, during the nonhunting months. At my suggestion of beans, Marion turns thumbs down. No way is she going to serve the Americans beans! Missionaries yes, but not strangers.

Since my suggestions are not helping her any, I take leave and head for the outside office to catch up on some paperwork, leaving her to figure out the menu as best as she can under these unusual circumstances. I know she will come up with something. She always does. When it comes to putting together a meal, Marion does wonders. I remember when we first started out often there were only pawpaws around to eat, which we were given for free when holding services on the estates along the escarpment. Marion managed to concoct several different dishes from them! She was even able to bake chiffon cake from an ostrich egg that was brought to our door. One of these is equivalent to two dozen chicken eggs!

Once before we had been without meat. But after we concluded our morning devotions, a small boy walked up to our door holding a leg of goat in his hand! He said that it was a gift from his father and mother. We now had meat. Maybe someone will come along again and bring us a leg of lamb.

During this time Marion is sharing her predicament with our house girls. They end up praying. Marion asks the Lord to help her know what to serve. Just recently she read of how the ravens had supplied Elijah with food. Surely the Lord is the same today! Could He not provide us with some meat as well?

It is midafternoon and I am still in my office when suddenly I hear Marion calling me rather excitedly, "Stan! Stan! Come quickly!" I rush to the door and glance towards the house. She and the girls are standing on the veranda in front of the kitchen door. Just below them on the lawn stands a bushbuck! There is a strange dog behind the animal barking and nipping at its heels.

I had heard a dog barking but chalked it up as one belonging to a Masai. Masai herd their cattle near the mission during certain times of the year, especially in the dry season. The boys who herd the cattle all have mangy dogs trailing along behind them. There were times when their cattle would have strayed onto the mission compound had I not prevented them. There is no fence or wall around our station.

The bushbuck does not move but keeps looking at Marion. I walk over to the animal and instantly notice the blood that is trickling down the hind legs where the dog bit them. I grab the bushbuck around the neck, and as soon as I do, the dog runs off into the bush. He does not return again. I do not even know who owns him.

What do I do now? The animal makes no move to bolt away but remains rooted to the spot. Marion exclaims, "Praise the Lord! He has provided the meat for us!" It now dawns on me that this is exactly what has happened! A dog shows up from nowhere, herds the wild animal up to our kitchen door, and then departs as soon as I have seized the bushbuck.

It is all very obvious that God has answered Marion's prayer for meat. He brought it right to her door? I butcher the bushbuck and the following day our company does eat meat—game meat, that is. Or "miracle meat," as Marion calls it! The Lord had again provided.

Chapter Eight

Signs and Wonders

Each weekend when Bible school is in session, students go out to witness on Saturdays and preach on Sundays. To begin with I accompany them. Then they travel in twos. Finally, when they have grown sufficiently in the Word and gained enough confidence in evangelism, they strike out alone. Eventually this leads to their pastoring a congregation either in Mbugwe or in Uburunge when Bible school closes down for several months.

Not everyone is gifted in preaching, and not everyone has a gift for singing. But there usually are a few who are talented in both fields. Fanuel is one of those who has a beautiful voice, either as a soloist or harmonizing with others in duets, trios, and quartettes. Many are converted under his ministry. As an evangelist he is one of the best.

One weekend finds Fanuel at Magara, one of our churches along the escarpment. It is Saturday evening and he is meeting with a handful of Christians in one of their huts. In spite of a *pombe* (native beer) party that is in progress nearby, they continue practicing songs for tomorrow's service. Their lusty singing soon drowns out the clamor of the drinkers around their beer pots. Those not too drunk withdraw themselves gradually and seek out the hut from where the hymns are flowing.

Then one of those already drunk jumps up and heads for

the hut where Fanuel and his group are rehearsing their songs. The drunkard is going to put an end to all of this singing, which has been interfering with his party. He pulls the knife from his belt and staggers through the doorway. Before any of those seated on the floor realize what is happening, the drunk lunges at Fanuel. The knife slashes the calf of one of Fanuel's legs, which he has raised hurriedly to protect himself.

The man quickly thrusts his knife again. Because of the excruciating pain in his leg, Fanuel is unable to react as he would like. He throws up his hands and the blade pierces the Swahili songbook, *Tenzi Za Rohoni*, which he is clutching in front of him. Those with Fanuel finally come to life and grab the drunken man from behind. They wrestle him to the floor of the hut and twist the knife from his hand. He is dragged outside and turned over to his comrades.

When Fanuel returns Sunday evening, he relates his near-escape from death. Marion inspects the wound that he received in his leg and dresses it properly. I am anxious to see the songbook. I had heard of a soldier in the Second World War who cheated death when a sniper's bullet hit the Bible the soldier carried in his shirt pocket. The bullet failed to pass through it, lodging at verse 7 in Psalm 91: "A thousand shall fall at thy side, and ten thousand at thy right hand, but it shall not come nigh thee."

The hole made by the drunkard's knife is there alright. It has pierced through most of the pages. But it did not go all the way through, fortunately. I look at the song where the knife stopped, and it is "Mikononi Mwa Yesu" ("Safe in the Arms of Jesus")! What a testimony! The Lord is telling us that Fanuel had been safe in His arms. It was He who had protected Fanuel from getting killed that night by a drunkard.

*   *   *

When we entered Uburunge, we first were given a plot at Aimabu to build our mission station. It is near the border of the Irangi tribe, who mainly are Muslims due to the influence of the early Arabs who settled along the slave route that ran through this area. We have come to evangelize the Waburunge people, who are animists, but here at Aimabu we also come face to face with the Muslims. Up to this point we have had several convert to Christianity, one of them being James Chimbalambala back in Mbugwe. Here in Kondoa District, the Islam faith is very strong. They oppose us at every turn at the district level, where the council is controlled by them, many of them being very militant and against Christianity.

I befriend one of our Muslim neighbours. His name is Salimu, and he accompanies me on many of my hunts for game meat. Often I allow him to administer the coup de grace, as their custom is that one of their kind must perform this in order for the meat to be eatable. Eventually he accepts the meat as being safe whenever I slaughter the animal, but not other "infidels," as Muslims call non-Muslims. Pork is taboo with them, so he will never touch a warthog or wild pig should one fall to my gun. He is an excellent tracker, and I discover this over and over when after the elusive greater kudu.

There are times we discuss the animistic practices of the Waburunge as well as the Christian faith that has come to this tribe. Salimu confesses that he is comfortable with his belief in Islam. It allows him to have more than one wife. "Thus far," he laughs, "I have four of them to do my work for me." But should Christianity present something supernatural, then he may be interested. To see that happen I tell him that he will have to attend our services, where Christ is preached. Will he accept the challenge?

One Sunday he appears in our yard and climbs onto the

back of our Jeep and rides along to the service at Aimabu, where we still meet in front of a hut. Salimu knows that what he is doing will not endear him to his fellow Muslims. But he has come to see. After we sing a few songs, I commence sharing the Word. A few minutes later, a women has an epileptic seizure. She falls to the ground at my feet. Immediately I stop preaching and start praying for her deliverance. In the rear of the group, sitting on a three-legged stool, is Salimu, spellbound.

He witnesses the healing of someone he has known to have had epilepsy for years. He has never seen this happen in the Islamic meetings he attended. It is a wonder! The sign of a supernatural act he had looked for he has now seen. No, we do not see him accept Christ, as we move back to Kaiti Mission in Mbugwe and lose touch with him. Our subsequent visits to Uburunge are made to Mirambo, where finally a plot has been granted for a mission station. But I leave Salimu knowing that he saw the power of Christ at work.

*   *   *

We discover that women, more than men, brew native beer in their villages throughout Mbugwe and Uburunge—especially the older ones. Millet or sorghum is cooked at the beginning of the week and then left to ferment for a few days. By Saturday it is ready for consumption. Neighbours start drifting in at nightfall, and before long the drums are heard both near and far. There is boisterous singing and lively dancing until the wee hours of the morning. If any beer is left over in the large clay pots or forty-five-gallon drum, then the drinking and dancing will resume Sunday evening.

Cooking beer is one of the leading vices, even ahead of committing adultery, that women wrestle with after accepting Christ. It is often their profession that they must give up. Their livelihood depends on the money received from the beer sold. Yet, according to Habakkuk 2:15–16: "Woe to him who gives drink to his neighbors, pouring it from the wineskin till they are drunk—you will be filled with shame instead of glory"! And so I remind them each opportunity I have, whether in church or at their homes, of God's Word against drunkenness, especially against those who bring it about.

A little old Mbugwe woman who faithfully cooks *pombe* regularly in Kaiti Village accepts Christ into her life. She forsakes her trade but after a few weeks begins to feel the loss of income from it. The temptation to return is too great, and she resumes cooking and selling *pombe* on weekends. We notice her absence at church and drive to her home. She does not have to admit it; the evidence is there for us to see. Clay pots are everywhere; one or two of them still contain the fermented millet brew.

She repents of her wrongdoing and comes back to church. It only is three weeks before she is back to brewing beer. Yes, she again repents and promises to follow Christ without fail this time. But, sadly, as before she is unable to leave her old business behind. It takes only two weeks this time around. She says to us, when we stop in after the service, "How do you expect me to get money for a dress? You want me to come naked to church?" I remind her that God cannot be mocked and a man reaps what he sows (Galatians 6:7). We leave her standing among her pots.

It is Saturday. Marion and I head into Arusha for our shopping. We leave early so that we can be back before dark. It is a hectic day, and we are ready for a bit of rest when we return home. Pulling into the mission, we find two men from the village waiting for us. They inform us that the little old lady who returned to brewing *pombe* is dead. She again had prepared beer for this weekend. Quite a few had already gathered to commence sampling it. When the drums began beating, she did something that she had not done for some time. She is the first one to walk into the circle of drinkers to start the dance. "The little old lady," says one of the men, "leaps up into the air and comes down dead!"

The two men beg me to come to the village, as everyone is in a state of fear. Those who were drinking are now on their knees begging God to spare them. The woman is still lying where she fell. All are afraid to touch her. They may be next! Would I come immediately to intercede on their behalf for God's forgiveness?

It is starting to get dark and I have had a full day, but this is not the reason that I refuse to accommodate the wrongdoers. I feel that this is a good time now for those at the *pombe* party to work things out between them and God. They may need all night to do it. As for the little old lady, she would not get buried until tomorrow anyway. She will do more good where she is right now than hidden away in the corner of a hut. And so I decline to go with the two men back to the village.

In the morning we make our way to the place of tragedy. To our surprise we discover the now-sober crowd still waiting for us. Not one of them slept a wink all night. Their faces show it—haggard and tired. I offer up a prayer, and then I ask them to move the dead woman inside the hut. She will be buried as soon as we sing a few hymns and I deliver the message. I do not have to elaborate much, as what transpired yesterday evening spoke more to them than any message I might bring. The sudden death of the woman as she prepared to dance was a sign to them that God cannot be mocked!

*   *   *

When darkness begins to settle upon the village of Magugu, Paulo stops hoeing his garden and commences to wend his way homeward. Off in the distance he sees patches of dust rising like mist above the brush that covers the surrounding countryside. Herds of cattle, intermingled with sheep, are being brought back from their grazing grounds near the Kilongozi River. The piercing whistles of the herders reach his ears. His own herd should be one of those returning home for the night.

No one greets Paulo when he reaches his *tembe* hut. Regina, his wife, is away visiting their daughter and will not be back for days. It is up to him to cook his meal, which he sets out to do. Soon the *ugali* is cooking over an open fire in a pot that is sitting on three large stones. His herdsman appears at the door just when the food is ready to be eaten. Before long they are gulping it down, as they have not eaten since morning.

Shortly after consuming their meal, they begin to feel pain searing their insides. When stomach cramps set in they are gripped with the horrifying realization that they have been poisoned! Before long the herdsman succumbs to death. A merciful release from the spasms that were racking his body. Paulo tries to rise to his feet and make it to the door in order to summon a neighbour for help. But he does not make it. He stumbles and falls towards the fireplace. His hands protect his face from the live coals as he sprawls flat on the mud floor. The unbearable pain he is suffering inside is now compounded by an added pain shooting up his arms from his hands stretched out in the fire.

Just as he is about to give up, two figures in white appear before him and proclaim, "Paulo, you will not die. We will help you." Having said this, they pull him away from the fire, and assist him through the door, which they have opened. Once outside, they deposit him on the ground and leave. Paulo now begins to heave and to vomit up his poisoned meal. It is here that a passerby discovers him, and soon neighbors are carrying him off to the nearby district hospital.

By morning word has reached the mission and Marion drives out to see the patient. She finds Paulo sitting up in bed, and he excitedly relates to her of his encounter with the angels who had come to save his life. During his stay in that hospital he boldly witnessed to everyone around him of his narrow escape from death. Thanks to those angels in white! Needless to say, Paulo was a faithful member of our church after that experience.

Who tried to kill Paulo? They had a suspect but no proof.

* * *

The Bible states: "And all liars, their place will be in the fiery lake of burning sulfur" (Revelations 21:8). Yet in spite of this grave warning, I have come across more transgressors in this sin than any other! Lying is all too common throughout the world. The rich do it, and the poor do it. The politician does it as well as most any man on the street. Working with Christians here, unhappily, I have witnessed all too often a lie following a previous transgression. It is not customary to reveal more than you have to. So, unless you catch him or her in the act of stealing or committing adultery or in a drunken stupor, an offender will resort to lying. In fact, should he convince you, through lying, that he is innocent, then he considers himself quite clever.

What about God in all of this? Oh, He will overlook their weaknesses. After all, it was the devil who made them do it! If you are going to blame anyone, it is him you need to hold responsible. *"Shauri ya Shetani"* ("Satan's issue") is commonly heard in Tanzania. As they take advantage of my own weaknesses, and it will not take them long to find these out, so, too, they take advantage of His love for mankind. In our eagerness to reveal that God is love, we fail to show them the other side of Him—His judgement and punishment of sin!

In the Old Testament we read of countless times when God punished wrongdoers immediately. Even in the Book of Acts we have the account of Ananias and Sapphira dropping dead because of lying. My previous account of the little old lady dropping dead at the *pombe* party for failing to abandon her occupation is an example of what can take place even today. The following incident concerns someone caught in a lie.

Reuben is a young Mbugwe. He recently accepted Christ, or so he says. Today he has come for some medicine. In his hand he is carrying a bottle of kerosene that he just bought at Mdori. In the course of the conversation, he is asked whether he has given up drinking. His answer is in the affirmative. To the astonishment of all those present, and especially Reuben, the bottle in his hand explodes and kerosene splatters all over him! He drops to his knees instantly and begs God to forgive him. God did not strike him dead for lying, as He did in the case of Ananias and Sapphira. But what He did was enough to bring the desired results. Reuben did more than just repent; he also decided to enroll in Bible school and eventually became one of our pastors.

*   *   *

Marion likes to serve bread, tea, and bananas to those who drop in at the mission. It is also a time to sit and visit with them. During these times, she learns much that assists her in dealing with their needs. During Bible school, the students are invited as well into our home to sample Marion's cooking and baking. Most of them have never eaten in a white man's home at a table with plates and silverware on it. They have to be instructed to pull up and place their feet underneath the table; otherwise they lose most of the food on their fork or spoon before it reaches their mouths.

Most Africans love bread, and so it is not strange that several Bible students ask Marion to teach them how to bake bread. She has them make a primitive stove out of a square four imperial-gallon tin container that kerosene is sold in at the *duka* (shop). The top or lid is cut open along three sides and now serves as a door when the container lies on its side. Once the dough is inside, the "stove" is then placed on top of stones that are nestled in live coals. Later, they learn to make a stove from a forty-five-gallon drum using the same method. Only now several loaves of bread can be baked at a time. Soon they are baking bread as good as Marion's.

There is one student whose bread turns out exceptionally well each time. Before long we hear that he is planning to go into business selling bread. Normally, we would be happy over such news, but this young man has had years of Bible school training and is an excellent preacher and teacher. Naaman has a great personality and certainly could go far in the ministry. We do not want to lose him. So we commence praying, asking God to spoil Naaman's bread if He wants him to continue in the ministry. If not, let him succeed.

A few days later, the dispenser from our clinic comes over to inform us that the last three times Naaman baked, the bread turned out so badly no one could eat it. He cannot understands what happened? It was so good before, and now it is spoiled each day he tries. We share with the dispenser how we had prayed about Naaman's intentions to set up a bakery, that if it is not God's will, then He should spoil Naaman's bread from now on. We now have our answer.

Naaman comes to see us and says that he has just learned from the dispenser that we have been praying about his baking bread. "Is it true?" he asks. We answer him that it is. I go on to share with him that we are concerned about him. God needs workers and he has been trained for that purpose. We pray together and he reconsecrates his life to serve the Lord in a greater way. He will again put Him first in his life.

* * *

Tithing, or giving a tenth of one's income for God's work, is never easy for most Christians all over the world. It is a principle, though, that needs to be practiced in order for the church to succeed in its programs. Because I exercise it, I initiate tithing in the churches and teach it during Bible school. It would be simple to excuse the poor, but if they fail to partake then God is unable to pass on a blessing to them. Jesus did not deny the poor widow giving out of her poverty (Mark 12:41–44). Therefore, no one is exempt. In fact, Jesus said, "Give, and it will be given to you, a good measure, pressed down, shaken together and running over, will be poured into your lap." (Luke 6:38).

To begin with, members invite us and the church leaders, during harvest season, to assist them in sorting out their one-tenth. The grain is then brought to the local church to be dedicated to God's work. It is Thanksgiving Day. Goats, chickens, and eggs end up at the altar as well. These are times that I will always remember with fondness. The workers in the mission compound have me deduct their tithe on pay day so as to make sure that God gets His share. When I believe that they have developed the habit, I ask them to start giving it on their own.

One of those workmen is Richard. He faithfully gives his one-tenth for some time. Then, he begins to withhold God's portion. I talk to him about it, reminding him of how God has been blessing him recently with a bumper crop of maize. But Richard not only fails to give his tithe from his salary; he also does not bring the tenth of his crop to church on Thanksgiving Day. I warn him that when God does not receive His due then we lose that portion anyway, for it does not belong to us.

Returning from a trip to Kenya, we discover Richard's kitchen, which he built behind his house, had caught fire and burned to the ground. All that he had stored inside, including his maize, perished! It is quite a loss. I do not have to tell Richard anything. He knows that he lost it because he had been withholding God's portion.

Francis also learns the hard way that to rob God is to invite misfortune. He is a deacon at one of the churches, and as soon as he understands the meaning of tithing, he commences to give the tenth of his crops to the church. When it comes to his livestock, though, it is more difficult for him to part with them. He has at least 300 sheep, plus goats and many cattle. Not only does the Lord say: "A tithe of everything from the land, whether grain from the soil or fruit from the trees, belongs to the Lord" (Leviticus 27:30), but He also says, "The entire tithe of the herd and flock, every tenth animal that passes under the shepherd's rod, will be holy to the Lord" (Leviticus 27:32).

We leave Francis to pray through his impasse. On the one hand, he knows it is his duty to give that tenth, but on the other hand, he lacks the consecration to go through with it. So often, it is the rich who find it difficult to bring to the Lord all of the tithe. One day, he shares with us that he will give the tenth of his flocks. But, after a couple of weeks, we fail to see him carry it out. Then comes the news that a disease has entered his flock of sheep. Before long, all 300 of them are dead and some of his goats.

Of course Francis laments the huge loss he has just suffered, but he acknowledges that it was the result of breaking his promise to God. Had he given away the thirty head of sheep to the Lord's work, he still would have been left with 270 head. Now he has none. Surely, to rob from God is to invite misfortune! (Malachi 3:8–11)!

Chapter Nine

Miracles

Marion and I have encountered numerous miracles during our years of ministry in Africa, many of them right here in Tanzania. Naturally, there were more miracles earlier on in our work. I believe the reason for this was so that the hearers would also *see* the hand of God and thus more readily believe the gospel. We read of this happening in the life of Jesus Christ himself. Signs and miracles abounded in the early stages of His ministry. This does not mean that He did not keep performing them until the close of His life on earth. But He did expect the hearers eventually to accept Him as the Saviour because of His message and not only for His miracles.

From the very beginning of our ministry in Africa, we learned to trust the Lord for all our needs, and that included our health. During our first five years we survived only because of our faith in the Almighty. We were far away from a doctor and hospital. Until we got to know the "lay of the land," we often failed to nourish our bodies as we ought to have. The Lord sustained us through those ill-prepared years. Marion and I have learned much since then, both spiritually and literally. The Scriptures have always been our teacher and guide and always shall be.

I have shared earlier in this book and in my previous one, *To a Land He Showed Us,* of healing and miracles that we have witnessed not only in our family, but in the lives of others as well. This chapter and the following one will contain more miracles, signs, and wonders that God performed in order that man may believe that He *is*.

* * *

The Wambugwe keep all livestock inside their flat-roofed houses. This is to protect them from lions and hyenas who may be hunting in the neighbourhood. And from the Masai warriors, who are ever on the prowl to increase their own herds. As a result, the Wambugwe live in constant danger of contracting tetanus from the plentiful manure in and around their homes. Should there be an open sore on someone's hand or foot, he or she is a likely candidate to catch this disease. This danger is very real, as the dung from the night is carried out to dry each morning and then returned as bedding in the evening.

We are called to one such hut early one morning. The message is that a man lies dying. Upon arrival, we find the animals have already vacated the premises and a crowd has assembled. The man is one of our Christians, and he has tetanus. An open wound near his ankle is infected. Just then, the sick man goes into spasms that rack his whole body. He utters no word, and upon a closer look, I discover his jaws are rigidly locked. No two answers are the same when I enquire as to how long the patient has been this way. He is an older man and lives alone most of the time.

This disease is usually fatal, especially once it has reached this stage. Several lift him up in order to move him outside to our vehicle. To my amazement, he is as stiff as a board! The muscles in his back are rigid, and when he begins to bow backwards, I order them to place him back on the cowskin. There is only one thing left to do out here in this remote area, and that is to ask God for assistance. It will take a miracle to heal the man! I do not see how else he can survive. The man is beyond human help.

His dry skin is cold to my touch when I place my hand on his chest to pray. After a few minutes of praying, I feel his heartbeat become fainter and then stop! Oh, no, is he dead? Under my hand I now feel goose bumps forming on his skin. There are sighs coming from the group assembled at the doorway. Those with me inside the hut have informed them that their friend is dead. They are whispering as to what to do with him now.

I cannot let this man die just like that in my presence! I bow my head again and call on God to give the Mbugwe back his life. It does not take long before the man gulps for air, to the utter amazement of those present! His heart begins to beat again, only stronger this time. The Lord has revived him and extended his life. A miracle? There is no other explanation of what just took place.

* * *

There is one more incident that I will share of how God again revived someone who was dead according to witnesses. But before I do, I wish to inform the readers that I have been reluctant to share these two incidents. Why? There are two reasons. First, many will not believe me. Second, those who do will ask me to raise their dead. After raising the daughter of Jairus, Jesus ordered the parents not to tell anyone what had happened. There are times when miracles are better left unrepeated, but not unrecorded.

Beside the Great North Road near our mission station is a borehole with a water trough. It was installed by the veterinary department years ago to assist the cattlemen. But, alas, the water is unfit for human or livestock consumption, for it is nothing more than a brownish brine. We found it even too salty for building purposes when we started on our mission station at Kaiti. In spite of its lack of use, the department still employs someone to take care of the premises. He pumps the troughs full with water so that his wife can wash their clothes and bathe the children.

Then one day there is an accident. The youngest child, just a toddler, falls into the water. The sister, who is a couple years older, runs to inform the mother. The father is not at home, as he has wandered off to Mdori, half a mile away. When the mother sees her baby submerged in the water, she goes into hysterics. At this very moment I am passing by on the Great North Road. I hear someone screaming and glance over in the direction from where the sound is coming and see a woman running towards me frantically waving her arms.

I stop my vehicle and wait for an explanation. She is hysterical, and it is difficult for me to understand her properly. But I finally am able to make out that her baby has drowned. I follow her to the water trough and discover the toddler still submerged in it. Scooping the child up into my arms, I find that there is no movement at all. Is the baby dead? How do you perform artificial respiration on someone so small? The mother looks at me pleadingly for help. What can I do?

With the child still clasped in my arms, I look up into the heavens and begin to pray. I ask the Lord to perform a miracle by restoring life to this little one. "The mother's heart is surely breaking; will You please hear this request?" I pray. The child stirs in my arms and I hand the mother her baby, who now is alive again. Praise the Lord! She showers her thanks on me, and I quickly take leave. I was getting embarrassed. Was it not God who performed the miracle?

The woman and I have met often since then, and each time she admits that had I not happened along just at that moment, her child would not be living today. Just before Marion and I left Tanzania, the parents came with their two daughters especially to say farewell and again to express their thanks for my part in the miracle that took place eleven years earlier!

*   *   *

There has been no rain to speak of in Mbugwe now for three seasons. It has been hot, dry, and dusty, day after day. As we look across alkaline flats we see shimmering mirages of lakes and in them float the square, low, flat huts. Carcasses of cows and wild animals lie scattered throughout the Rift Valley. People have died, some of them old, others just children. Any food that can be found in the far-off forests is quickly eaten by the stronger in the village. The survival of the fittest!

The United States has sent relief. But only those who are able to walk to the distributing centers will receive a ration of corn. In our immediate vicinity we are left with those who are not receiving any assistance. We never send anyone away, but give them beans and *posho* (cornmeal) when they come to the mission. We deliver the food to those who are unable to trudge their way to our door. This has been a time of learning to share, a time of opening our cupboards and our hearts to a people who are existing by dividing out their rations to see how long they can make them last. Often they eat but once every two days!

Then the rains finally come. Wonderful, glorious rain! These skinny, skin-stretched-over-bones Wambugwe rush out to their gardens and commence hoeing and planting maize and millet. Before long, their crops are growing nicely. There is hope once more of having some food. When the grain is in the crucial growing stage, the rains stop. Days stretch into weeks and the rains do not resume. Rainmakers and witch doctors are out trying to conjure up rain to save the crops. But to no avail.

Today is the day that Marion is travelling out to Mwada to join the ladies in their weekly Bible study. When she arrives, she makes for the tree where they usually meet. While waiting for the women to arrive, she gazes around her at the maize and millet, which is beginning to wilt. Up above her is a cloudless sky! She knows that if there is no rain in the next few days, the crops will be beyond saving.

Marion looks at the lesson she has prepared and realizes that this is not what is needed today. How can I tell them that God loves them when they have suffered so in the past three seasons? Barely surviving and losing many of their families through hunger. As the ladies gather around her God gives Marion a new message. She opens the Bible to 1 Kings 18:16–46 and relates to them about Elijah on Mount Carrel, all about the contest between Baal and God. The rain had come because Elijah prayed and believed it would come. He did not give up!

When she has concluded her lesson, Marion reminds them that the witch doctors have been defeated in bringing rain to Mbugwe. "Whom should you trust in to bring us rain?" she asks them.

Their reply is: "It is God Who will bring us rain." They all kneel under the tree, in the dust, and start to call on God. There is much weeping as they seek the Lord. They pray with the Psalmist, "Hear my prayer, O Lord, and let my cry come onto you. Do not hide your face from me in the day of trouble."

Having concluded their prayers, they feel their burdens have been lifted. They arise assured that God will take care of everything. One of the women invites them into her *tembe* hut. Before stooping over in order to enter through the low doorway, Marion looks up at the sky. Not a cloud in sight. Once she is inside, the ladies share their problems with the missionary. They chat and eat the hard kernels of maize that have been roasting in the smoldering ashes. All are enjoying this time of fellowship. There is even laughter. Time passes on.

There are no windows, only a small peephole here and there, so the women are unaware of what is happening outside. Clouds have been gathering, and when Marion steps outside the first drops of rain fall on her upturned face from the darkening sky above. What excitement! What rejoicing! They all stand with hands raised towards heaven, praising the Lord. The rain is coming more rapidly. The Wambugwe are getting soaked to the skin, but they do not mind. They are singing and dancing in the rain.

Marion rushes to the car. She has to get going, and drives all the way home in pouring rain. It continues to rain for three days! The crops are saved. Praise God from whom all blessings flow! To this day these women know that it was God Who heard them and sent the rain. As He had performed a miracle for Elijah, so He also did for Marion and the women of Mwada one cloudless day. The Word does say that if we cry onto God, He will hear us. Amen!

*   *   *

We returned from our second furlough with a set of 16mm films on the life of Christ that we then commenced showing at many of our churches in Mbugwe and in Uburunge. Before long I had them translated into the Swahili language onto audiotapes, which then were plugged into the projector so that they could hear their language instead of English. It was a first for most of them to see moving pictures. Many who had never attended any of our services now come to see and hear the gospel. It was an eye-opener to us as well to notice those who laughed during somber moments on the film. How different from our reactions!

Even the Masai from nearby *manyattas* (enclosed homesteads) allow their curiosity to get the better of them and wander over to view the films. I will never forget the time we showed some warriors our 8mm movie films we had taken of them. They laughed at each other and then at themselves. There actually was nothing humorous on the film, but the warriors just found it too comical to see and hear themselves and ended up rolling on the ground with laughter!

Revival meetings follow the showing of the films on Christ. Not only do I go out preaching in the evening services, but pastors with the gift of evangelism do as well. As a result, churches are strengthened and their membership increases. Marion holds weekend seminars with the women at many of the churches in Mbugwe. The ladies here and in Uburunge take longer to leave their traditional beliefs behind and follow Christ without looking back. She has exciting times with them. Not only do they learn from her, but she also learns from them.

This weekend finds Marion at Osoley, where the pastor is Boniface, the husband of Angelina who worked for us in the house. There are many Wambugwe residing in this rather picturesque area. Sangaiwe Ridge separates them from the Ntarangire National Park. Yet there are wild animals that roam about freely, especially at night. It is here that the original Wambugwe once settled about two hundred years ago, but when plagued with chiggers and marauding Masai, they moved onto the alkaline flats. There the Wambugwe lived until recently, when the government forced many of them back to this area.

Baobab trees are scattered throughout the countryside. Herds of cattle search for grass along the ridge and roam as far north as Lake Burungi. The eerie howl of the hyena greets you as darkness closes in. Once night has fallen, the low grunt of the lion breaks the stillness and no one moves around freely anymore. Recently one did, and he was mauled to death. Only the elephant ignores the king of beasts as his high-pitched scream floats down from the ridge above. Against this wild, yet exciting, background Marion is preparing to conduct a service with the inhabitants of Osoley.

Earlier in the day, she had met with the women in the church and taught them from the Word of God. It was decided then to also hold an evening service. But a large bonfire would have to be made in order to attract the villagers. There was a problem, though. In this area, as soon as it gets dark, the wind comes alive. "It is so strong," says Boniface, "that it is impossible to have a fire." But the more Marion thinks about it, the more she feels that they should go ahead and plan the service with a bonfire.

She enters the church and begins talking with the Lord. She asks Him to still the wind and to bring out the people so that they can get to know Him. Marion then stands on Matthew 7:7–8: "Ask and it will be given to you, seek and you will find, knock and the door will be opened to you. For everyone who asks receives, he who seeks finds; and to him who knocks, the door will be opened."

After the evening meal of *ugali* and chicken prepared by Angelina especially for Mama, they set out preparing the place of worship. The wind has already started to blow when the *kuni* (firewood) is gathered and piled near the church. All the three-legged stools available, plus the chairs from the pastor's house, are carried to the site. Sure enough, the wind is increasing in volume as Boniface had predicted. "There is no way we can have this fire," he states.

But Marion keeps standing on the Word, even when darkness engulfs them as quickly as one pulls the shade of a window. She knows the time has now come to prove the Lord herewith. The wind is making itself known quite forcibly, but she believes that God has control over it. She asks Boniface to strike the match. Immediately the wind ceases! Praise the Lord!

Well, they go ahead and hold the service. Many come when they see the huge bonfire light up the sky. The Wambugwe at Osoley not only hear Marion preach about trusting in Jesus Christ, but they also hear the pastor, who cannot say enough of how God took care of the wind!

*   *   *

Chapter Ten

The Complexities of Marriage

Parents arrange the marriages here. When the son is of age, his father goes about choosing a girl for him. As soon as the boy's father has found her, he sits down with her father to discuss the prospects of their two children getting married. If the outcome is a positive one, the boy's father returns home and sends over several head of cattle. They are there for only a day and then brought back. The following day, he sends someone to ask the girl's father whether he found the cattle satisfactory. Were they large enough, fat enough, and numerically enough? If the answer that comes back is in the affirmative, then the cattle are driven again to the girl's father in a day or two. This time they stay. Once the dowry has been received, the wedding can now take place.

What about the young couple? They have as yet not met! In Mbugwe, they eventually do the evening before the wedding. Their first meeting takes place in the dark room of a hut. Here they stay until morning. It is then that the parents arrive to check on whether they fared well. If they did, then the wedding is on.

There are times that the young man will attempt to secretly view the girl he is to marry. This happens frequently in Uburunge. He is curious to know whether she has a good nature and is a hard worker. The girl is unaware that she is being spied upon. But many of the young men in Uburunge do not know whether their brides are disabled or strong, sickly or healthy, until the day they are carried over to the grooms' hut, on the shoulders of the boys' young friends on the day of the wedding. This custom of transporting the girl to the young man's house is not practiced in Mbugwe.

I wish to interject here that on several occasions I have stood in for the young man's father and talked to the girl's father concerning the dowry. They were Bible students from outside Mbugwe wishing to marry one of the local girls who called on me to assist them. I like to believe that I did quite well in getting the old man to lower the bride price. My argument was that it was the mission that was educating the girl. Therefore, we should be receiving a portion as well. The father usually sees the point and lowers the dowry. But there is a lot of jawing before an agreement is finally reached. You cannot rush through something important like this!

The marriage may proceed quite smoothly for three or four years. But then, if the husband fails to produce a bull, which is called *Kesengeliko,* to celebrate with her parents, she will become rebellious. This bull is not part of the dowry. It is a gift given in appreciation for their daughter, a thank-you to the parents. *Kesengeliko* secures the marriage. The bull is slaughtered, and a feast takes place. Without this happening, the wife will feel unappreciated. The result is that she will desert the husband and return to her parents. Not because of any argument, but because he did not give *Kesengeliko.* If after some time the husband still fails to oblige, the marriage will dissolve completely.

During this time, the parents no longer have authority over their daughter. Since she has fulfilled her abstention period from her first husband, brought about by this custom, she now is free to choose her own destiny. She is soon married by someone else, not once, but often after that, especially if she is able to bear children with each man. The dowry is cancelled in each marriage when she has produced children, and it does not have to be returned by her parents. She can release herself to marry another man and to repeat the same thing over again. The father who is after wealth will not object to her life-style. Does she not fetch him some riches?

Through this process she also acquires wealth along the way, as the children belong to her and her parents in Mbugwe society. Should one of her ex-husbands pass away, her children will inherit their share. Inheritance follows the maternal line. The child bears the surname on the mother's side of the family. When her current husband dies, she and the children obtain the property. Thus, women who have some substance have traded their bodies for it. Many have lived with ten or more men during their married years.

Marriage is doomed to fail, as the girl, from the very beginning to the time of the wedding, has no input. The father, who is anxious for the bride price, plans it all. He does not give her time to grow up and choose her own lover. Instead, she may end up married to a miser or someone much older than herself. Should the husband be too old to suffice her, she will be tempted to look elsewhere for some affection. Wherever she travels with him, those of her own age will tease her that he is her father.

Eventually, she will leave him and the marriage that was planned so well by the parents is now broken. The girl who had a difficult life at home, and then with her first marriage, will now seek an easier life with someone her own age. But it may not stop with the next marriage. In her newfound freedom she will be tempted, as I mentioned earlier, to follow the trail of trading her body for wealth.

We are thankful that the teachings of Jesus Christ are making a difference with many marriages that were arranged under Christian guidance. There is hope for the girls that they will get an opportunity to have a say in choosing their husbands and that their marriages will take place because of the couple's love for each other. The government is also stepping in to change the ancestral bloodline from the mother to the father. This should check any attempt by women whose aim it is to marry and remarry for the purpose of acquiring more wealth.

As well, the government is assisting the church in teaching against forcing young girls into early marriages. Among the Wanyaturu, in Singida District, the girls are betrothed as soon as they are born! The man will pay the dowry when his "bride" is old enough to carry water and build a fire for cooking. She moves in with him at the early age of six or seven. There she works for him and may not have intercourse with him until she reaches adolescence.

*　　*　　*

Soon after our arrival in Tanganyika, Marion is called upon to assist women in delivering their babies. One of the first cases are twins. Marion never had experience in this sort of thing before coming to Africa. But once here, she cannot come up with enough excuses not to help them. Before long she is sought after to deliver babies throughout Mbugwe. Why? Because of God lending a hand, she does not lose a single baby!

Marion is called to their homes at all hours. When it is after dark, I drive with her out to the expecting mother's hut. While Marion is inside about her duties, I lounge outside and listen to the sounds of the night. Something disturbs a nearby nightjar. Its high-pitched call startles the mongrel dozing at the corner of the hut. He does not bark, probably recognizing no threat in that sound. But he does yelp a few times when a hyena starts to howl out on the flats. He is joined by another hyena only a stone's throw away from where I sit. It is pitch-dark. Then a scream pierces the air! It comes from inside the hut. Marion has just delivered another baby! If it is a girl, then she will probably be named Marion. If a boy, then he may have Hoffman for a name. There are a few Stanleys around, more in Uburunge. As for Marion, she has quite a few named after her. One mother in Mbugwe named both of her girls that Marion helped to deliver Marion. (The second one had come along a few years later.)

It is quite difficult at times to assist the expectant mother in the delivering of her baby. There are always older women present who wish to force their often very primitive methods to bring about childbirth. When Marion is called to the village, she already knows that the women have failed in their efforts. That is why they have sent for her. The woman in labor is completely exhausted. She is quivering and her limbs are cramped from her being forced to squat on her haunches for hours. Marion scolds the old local midwife for her cruel tactics and lays the young woman back on the cowskin, then commences to gently massage her muscles. It works and before long the baby is born. Had Marion not showed up when she did, the young woman may have died at childbirth as many of them do in similar cases.

Girls who worked for us on the mission usually have Marion do the honours after they are married and are raising a family. They either come to have their babies here on the station or invite Marion to their homes. There are times when the cases are too complicated for her and she drives them to the hospital at Magugu or to Dareda should it be very severe. Once she just makes it to the hospital in time, but not the delivery room. The woman has her baby on the doorstep! The twenty miles of corrugated road were just too much.

Marion takes every opportunity she can get to teach these young Christian women who are expecting children to drop harmful practices in their traditional beliefs. They will be pressured from their pagan mothers and grandmothers to observe these customs, but they are to stand firm in their newfound faith.

She reminds them that when the baby has swollen gums and cries a lot, it is not because of a worm in there that is causing it. The baby is only teething, and the whiteness they see in the gum is a new tooth forming. But their medicine man will tell them that it is a *dudu* (worm) that needs to be removed, which he then does by digging it out with a sharp piece of rusty wire that has a hook at the end.

Marion also teaches them not to remove the baby's two lower front teeth, which many were doing after the child was weaned. This is done so that the child can be fed through this gap should lockjaw occur. Tetanus is quite common due to the unsanitary surroundings children find themselves in their homes. Livestock is kept indoors for the night under the same roof. The stench of the raw manure is nearly unbearable, and the flies are numerous. Any scratch becomes a candidate for this death-threatening disease. The answer lies in prevention, treating the wounds immediately, Marion instructs them. Not in knocking out the front teeth, which at best, because of the food they are receiving, prevents death for a short time only.

There is also the custom of their tribal markings, which are slashes across each cheek bone. This scarification is usually performed by the grandmother when the child has been weaned. It was very upsetting for Marion to receive the news that a child who had been named after her had been subjected to this tribal tattooing after the mother had promised she would not do it. This rite may have served a purpose during the age of strong tribal ties, but now with nationalism being taught, it has no place in society.

There is one delivery she makes that we both will remember, especially Marion. It is at the end of the rainy season. Our river has flooded its banks, and there is knee-deep water all the way to the houses on the other side. The road to the highway is too muddy for our vehicle, and so it is parked half a mile away on some high ground. On our side of the river we slush around in rubber boots.

It is during this time that Romonah, now married to Eliezer, is expecting her second child. With her first one, Marion had to take her to the hospital. Now with this one, she is determined to have it at the mission. But Marion is prepared to take her to the hospital again should it be necessary. The only thing she asks of Romonah is that she warn her in plenty of time so that they both can make it to the vehicle before she goes into heavy labor.

It is 11:00 P.M. and there is rain outside. Marion and I are awakened with a *"Hodi."* coming through our open window. It is Romonah and Eliezer. She is in labor. She could not have picked a worse time! Marion invites them inside and asks her if she can make it to the vehicle near the main road. But Romonah declares, "I am now ready."

What to do? Marion begins to panic! There is no time to walk Romonah to the vehicle in pouring rain over a muddy and slippery road. She could deliver along the way. No, she will have to be attended to in our house. This is going to be a first for Marion! No women to assist her with the delivery. She exclaims to Romonah, "You know I have never done this alone before!"

The reply is, "Between you and me, and God, we can do it."

Thus assured, Marion offers up a prayer that God will help her so that all will go well.

I am called into action as well. While still in Canada, Marion had heard that a lot of hot water was needed for childbirth, so she asks me to prepare some. Then she sterilizes the utensils she will be using. Colleen, our daughter, is moved out of her bedroom onto the couch in the living room. Her room will now serve as the delivery room. Soon Romonah is occupying Colleen's bed. The labor pains are now almost constant. Eliezer has returned to their place across the river.

While Marion is encouraging Romonah, I am pouring water into her mouth to keep her from dehydrating, as she is having a rough time. Then the baby arrives and it is another girl. Marion passes her on to me while she takes care of Romonah. I hang on to the little bundle until Marion finally comes to tend to her. Everything went smoothly. Marion did an excellent job! When it is all over she steps outside to bring up her evening meal. It is now midnight.

Returning inside, Marion notices the hot water still on the stove. Now what was all that water for anyway? She will have to find out when she gets back to Canada. Turning to me, she says, "Call Eliezer and we will all enjoy a cup of tea. There is plenty of hot water." Romonah and the baby stay with us for five days before she wades back across the river to her house. What is the name they give their daughter? It is Colleen.

A few years later, when we have opened our own clinic here on the mission, Romonah is in charge of the delivery room. She is an excellent midwife. Many babies are escorted into this world with her assistance. As for Marion, she now can rest from the practice of delivering babies in Mbugwe. God has been able to use her, in spite of her being a very delicate person who used to faint easily at the sight of blood. She gives God the glory for the strength and grace He gave her in those awkward times.

I need to mention here that not every woman in Mbugwe can conceive and bear children. In fact, when we first came here we learned that the population was in a decline! There were several reasons for that, we learned. The high rate of bilharzia in this tribe was unbelievable. Medical programs helped eventually to bring the level down considerably. Venereal disease ran rampant in Mbugwe. The message of salvation aided medicine in reversing its growth.

A major reason, I believe, that young women fail to conceive is the sex life that they have had at a very early age. The girls are circumcised when they reach the age of puberty. After this they are considered eligible for marriage. But there are those who have had sexual intercourse long before this. It gets worse after circumcision, for now the ability to reach a climax has been lessened, forcing her to seek out lovers at an all-night *ngoma* (dance) for fulfillment. It does not take long in living a life like this before she has ruined her capacity to conceive.

Many women have been married several times. One admitted to Marion that she has lived with at least twenty different men already! When the woman cannot bear a child after two to three years, then she is discarded for another one. The dowry, or bride price, for her is lowered after each divorce until she can be married for only a pittance. Her womanhood suffers greatly, and in the end she is left to live out her life alone.

It does not take long before we discover that several wives of our pastors are unable to bear children. They come to Marion, one by one, to disclose their plight. "Is there any help?" they ask her.

"Well, yes and no," she answers, and then goes on to explain. "If you are diseased inside, then the doctor may be able to treat you, but if you are barren, then only God can help you." The women agree to be examined by a doctor, and Marion transports them to one in Arusha. What will the answer be?

The doctor finds half of them to be treatable. The rest are either fertile or barren. Those who learn they are capable of bearing children are ecstatic. But the problem is not yet over for them. This means that their husbands may be sterile!

No man in Africa will ever admit to being unproductive. It is always the woman's fault. Sure enough, when the men are confronted with the news, they are not willing to go for a checkup. They are afraid of the results. And so it is not long before one of them leaves his wife for another woman who already has children.

What about those who have had their fears confirmed that they are barren? The only help for them now is, as Marion told them earlier, if God would perform a miracle and open their wombs! Childlessness is a curse out here. As it was in the days of Sarah and Hannah in the Old Testament, so it is still in many parts of the world today. The woman bears the brunt of the shame that comes with being barren.

It is often after this that we are called upon to pray for those who have no children and yet would like to conceive. Marion and I lay our hands on the women, most of them very young, and ask God to grant them their wishes. He does. Each one of them conceives and in the appointed time brings forth a child. The proud mothers then carry their babies to church and dedicate them to the Lord. We rejoice with them for answered prayer.

Helena is the wife of one of our pastors in Mbugwe. They have no children and are both up in years. She was one of those that Marion took to the doctor for an examination. Her hopes were dashed when she learned that she was unable to bear a child. In fact, she was told that she was past the time of bearing children! Will her husband continue to keep her, now that the truth is out? Will his profession as a Christian be strong enough to keep him from following the old ways? Or will he yield and look for a younger woman?

Six months pass by. Then, one day, Marion has a caller. It is Helena. As soon as she is seated, she begins to weep. Slowly she shares her grief. "My husband has told me today that he is going to send me away and look for another woman who is able to bear him a child." He said that he cannot wait any longer. "What can I do now? I have failed him," she adds.

Marion relates to her the stories from the Bible of Sarah and Hannah and reminds Helena that God is able to perform a miracle in her life as well. He is no respecter of persons! All that is needed is faith in Him that He will hear her cry and give her the longed-for child. As Marion keeps talking to her, she can feel Helena's faith increasing. When she is ready for prayer, my wife calls me and we anoint her with oil. We beseech the Lord to grant her a child as He had Sarah and Hannah before her. After prayer, Helena leaves us. Not as she came, but full of joy, expecting God to answer her prayer.

We make a trip to see her husband and inform him that he should not act hastily, but persevere, as God is going to reward him if he keeps serving Him. We pray with Neman, and he gives us his word that he will not dismiss his wife. Soon, the members in the church learn of Helena's journey to the mission for prayer so she can conceive and bear a child, even in her later years. "Will God perform a miracle for her?" is on their lips.

Yes, He heard her cry and Helena conceives. There is rejoicing in their home. The unbelievable has happened! Once when complications set in, her faith is severely tested. She comes to the mission, and Marion tends to her. After some bedrest, she recuperates and returns home. Will she be able to carry the baby the full nine month? We pray that she will. Surely the Lord is able to complete the work He has begun in her.

Marion is called at night to deliver a baby of the wife whose husband works for the mission. It is a boy, healthy and strong. She just arrives home in the morning when another caller comes for her. Marion goes and this time she delivers a baby girl. It is afternoon when she pulls into the yard. But this is not the end yet. A message arrives asking that she come immediately to assist Helena, as she is ready to deliver her child.

Although tired, Marion crawls back into the vehicle and heads out to Neman and Helena's home. She is praying all the way there that God will give an easy delivery. He does hear her and Helena gives birth to a healthy baby boy! Praise the Lord! They name him Imanueli—gift of God. For surely he is a gift from God!

Helena does not bear another child. God knows what He was doing when He granted her that one child be a boy. Had it been a girl, then Neman would not have had an heir, thus would wish for another child. But now the desire of his heart had been granted—to have a son. And hers was granted as well—to have a child.

Chapter Eleven

Recollections

Throughout the years in Tanzania the thought of leaving one day had never really crossed my mind. When Marion and I first came here, it was to stay. I often said to the Wambugwe that after I died, they were to bury me on top of one pyramidal hill, preferably on the south side of the third one, where my grave could look out onto the valley below. But that unthinkable day has come! It has come to shatter any further dreams I may have had for the work here in Tanzania. Time to set my feet on new territory for the Lord has finally run out. No more tracks in the dust!

It has been fifteen years now since Marion and I set foot here in the country. Yet it feels like only yesterday. It is here that we learned to walk and live by faith. What exciting years they were! We came here having had no previous experience in the mission field. No one was waiting for us to show the new couple the ins and outs, the dos and don'ts, of missions. But we had a call and the faith necessary to not only survive in this harsh environment, but also to pioneer a work for the Church of God in Tanzania.

In the beginning it often was by trial and error that we learned and gained knowledge. These experiences, unknown to us at the time, were to assist us greatly in pioneering and establishing future works in other lands. It takes years to mature, or should I say to develop, into a servant fit for the

Master's use. These years in Tanzania provided that opportunity for Marion and me to exercise our faith, more so than had we stayed home in Canada to pastor a church. Thank you, Lord, for the training we have had here for the past fifteen years!

Not only am I leaving wiser than when I came, but also with memories that time will not erase. Should they grow dim in years to come, my diaries will surely remind me and I will relive them again. Another reminder of my years here is a thorn in my flesh. Yes, that is what I said, a thorn in my flesh! Not the kind that the Apostle Paul had, but a real one. It is still there where it lodged in my right forearm in 1968.

It happened one afternoon while I was assisting the workmen in cleaning away thorn trees on the plot of ground at Mirambo where we had commenced erecting the mission station in Uburunge. As I was limbing the tree that I had just felled, one of the branches sprang back and drove a two-inch thorn into the muscle of my right forearm. The pain was excruciating! As I tried to remove myself from the thorny branch, the thorn stripped off at the base. All two inches was now lodged deep inside my muscle. Since the thorn entered point-blank, I believed it could be withdrawn simply by seizing the stub end of it and pulling. But it was not to be. The thorn held tight. After a few attempts, the skin slipped over the remaining part and I had to give up. We already had our dispensary operating on the station, and I made my way to it. Ezekiel's attempts to extract the thorn with tweezers failed as well. Next he made an incision in order to get at the thorn as the end kept breaking off, but all to no avail. He finally gave up, afraid he might damage the muscle should he continue probing. And about time! My arm was on fire. I drove back to Aimabu, where we were staying while with the Waburunge.

I could not use my right hand for anything much for months. Each time I tried, the thorn in my flesh reminded me that it was there by sending a sharp pain up my arm. Even writing and lacing my shoes were impossibilities. I could feel the sharp end of the thorn where it almost reappeared after having passed through the muscle and flesh. Bending the last three fingers is what caused all the pain until finally the arm adjusted to the intruder.

During a trip up to western Kenya, I dropped in to see Dr. Anderson at Mwihila Mission. After an X ray of my arm, he concluded that the thorn should stay where it is. Cartilage had already formed around it, and soon the thorn would be imbedded in it. In time it might even be dissolved. To try to remove the thorn surgically could endanger the usage of some fingers should a muscle or nerve get severed, he added. And so today, as I ponder our departure, I can still find that thorn in my flesh.

While it was easier for me to settle into our new life in Africa, especially here in Mbugwe, it was not so with Marion in the beginning. Her life in Canada was much different than mine. She got the chance to taste the finer side of life as she climbed the ladder in society. I remained in rural Saskatchewan until the day I left to enter the ministry. And even then the country went with me. So it was not that difficult for me to accept the Tanganyika bush, the wildlife, the primitive native, the hot climate, the annoying insects, and the lack of so many things that make a house a home.

Her victory finally came through much prayer and seeking God's face. The day finally came when she could say to the local inhabitants who called at the door, *"Karibu"* ("Come in"), instead of *"Unataka nini?"* ("What do you want?") It was more of a sacrifice for Marion than for me to bond with those we had come to evangelize. The women were very backward, and their conversation centered around bearing children and how mean their husbands were to them. Not exactly the kind of companionship Marion was used to. Where others may have given up, her determination to love the unlovely came out on top finally.

God not only gave her the love that she needed, but He also endowed her with compassion to help others in their needs. There was no disease that she did not try to treat. Thus someone who had fainted at the sight of blood now had the stomach to dress rotting ulcers, remove maggots from infected ears and infested wounds, and deliver babies, which I have mentioned earlier. The old women that she earlier had found unpleasant she now discovers are charming in their own special way.

Whenever we spent some time at Aimabu, an old lady was sure to drop in to greet us. She appeared to be in her late eighties, but women age rapidly here in Africa. How old she really was even she could not tell us. What hair she still had was white and woolly. Her face was covered with wrinkles, and there was not a tooth left in her mouth. Tobacco had stained her nose from sniffing it for years. She still liked to wear beads around her neck, and they also hung from her ears. Amazingly, her sight, in spite of cataracts, sufficed for her to move about freely.

One day, as we were returning to Aimabu from Goima, we met our lady friend going the same direction. We stopped and offered her a lift. But after only a short distance, the men in the back had all they could do to keep her from leaping off the pickup! It was her first ride on a moving vehicle, and it scared her silly to see trees flying by. I had to stop and they lowered her back down to familiar territory, where trees stood still and the ground did not move. We left the old woman to finish her journey as she had done it all her life—shuffling along slowly, stooped over her walking stick, with a soiled cloth for a wraparound.

A young girl, one of her great-grandchildren, always came with the old woman on her visits. On one occasion she informed us that she had many more of them and asked if I could relieve her of one or two of the girls. I declined. Marion had many chats with her and from them learned much of their tribal customs. She also discovered that the old lady had a keen sense of humour. But when it came to discussing eternity and the need for her to accept Christ, she would give us that toothless grin and simply reply that she was going to the place of her ancestors. She wished to be with them.

We did not see her accept Christ. Had we stayed on at Aimabu instead of making Mirambo our place of abode when in Uburunge, then we might have seen it happen, as it did with many others. There is Maria at Goima, an old woman, paralyzed in both legs, who has to be carried or else crawl in order to get around. She accepted Christ when we planted a church in her village. Even though God did not see fit to heal her, she continues to live for Him in spite of her handicap. God has rewarded her by giving her several dreams and visions. Most of them were warnings for different members in the church.

I need to mention another old woman, well up in years, who visited Marion quite often at Kaiti, for she lives in Mbugwe. She resembles the old lady at Aimabu in many ways, except she has a tooth or two. She is Kaderiya, Angelina's grandmother, caught up in witchcraft since childhood until the day she came in contact with our church through her granddaughter. Since becoming a Christian, Kaderiya is a joy to be with. For an old lady, her sense of humour has no equal. Marion found Kaderiya a joy to visit with.

I also recollect Zilipa's aging father, Lee, who is now in his nineties and almost totally blind. On our last visit to Uburunge, I dropped in to say farewell to him. He could not believe that I was leaving and he would never see me again. I reminded him that should he accept Christ, we will meet again. He said that he does want to be with God as well when

108

he dies and right there he asked me to pray for him. What a miracle to see this old man, a witch doctor all his life, snatched in the nick of time from everlasting punishment!

There are many more that I could mention here, but will not, who had a chance to hear the gospel during their lifetime because of our presence in this land. Thousands have accepted Christ under our ministry during the past fifteen years. Not only did we plant churches in Mbugwe and Uburunge, but also the Word was preached to the Masai at the nearby *manyattas*. The Word was also carried to the Wanyiramba and the Wanyaturu in Singida District, and churches sprang up there.

The Nyaturu tribe is noted for a secret cult called the Lion Men, who terrorized villages in years past. Witches sought out young victims and hid them in caves where their limbs were broken and then reset so that after they mended they would walk on all fours. During this whole process they were under a spell and taught to roar like lions. When the time came to send them forth on a mission of death, a lionskin was draped over each one and the claws attached to their limbs. Thank God this cult no longer exists today!

In 1968 the Farmers went on furlough. During their absence, I made several trips to supervise the work in Mbulu District and shared the gospel with the Wambulu (Iraqw). They are Hamites, the same as the Waburunge. We carried on in visiting the church in Yaida Valley, where the Watindiga, who are Bushmen, live. They are a small tribe and gradually getting smaller. I have hunted down here on numerous occasions, especially for elephants. Those memories linger on.

It is here in Tanzania that I cut my teeth in hunting big game. Many of those adventures have been recorded in my book *In the Tanganyika Bush*. As any kid growing up in Africa learns to hunt, so also have mine. Mark is just beginning, but as for Colleen and Kirk, they have developed into crack shots.

Many an animal has fallen after being hit only once. Will Kenya hold for us as well the thrill of the hunt and then the conquest?

It was exciting to witness some of the scenes as they were being filmed for the movie *Hatari*, starring John Wayne. We often met him in the hotel dining room where we ate our noonday meal when shopping in Arusha. While we were watching a scene with John Wayne in it on one of the streets, the movie crew moved all of us back except for three women. One of them was Marion. After this our children dubbed her one of John Wayne's leading ladies in *Hatari*. Some of the animals captured in that film were caught near our place.

The years have slipped by quickly, too quickly! I suppose because there was always something to do. If we weren't teaching in Bible school, then we were holding classes for the youth or for the women. When the mission board requested that we run only one Bible school in Tanzania and chose the one at Mbulu to be it, I started the Theological Education by Extension (TEE) program a year later to meet the need for training leaders here in Mbugwe. Prior to its closure, Kaiti Bible School had existed for thirteen precious years. Marion and I taught in it during that whole time. Many pastors got their start there.

Marion has been faithful in publishing the *Mpanzi* (the *Sower*), a periodical she started back in 1966. It contains a message, testimonies, announcements, and news of interest for Uburunge and Mbugwe. She is turning it over to Eliezer, who will endeavour to carry it on after our departure. The past two years I have been busily preparing a Swahili hymnal that will be used by the church not only here in Tanzania, but throughout East Africa. It involved translating 100 new songs from our English hymnal, plus revising some of those already in Kiswahili.

These past three years have been the most convenient for

us since we started. We now have a light generating plant that Marion can switch on while in the house. She no longer has to go out to the shed where it is kept to switch it off at night when I am not there to do it. There was always the danger of stepping on a snake or meeting a leopard in the dark, so one had to sprint right smartly to enter the house before the light died out completely. If we did not want to do that then we had to carry a torch holding excellent cells.

There is now a line of communication to the outside world. No, not a telephone, but a radio that we use to call Arusha and then it is relayed to anyone with another radio or telephone. We are able to contact the children at Rift Valley Academy (RVA) at regular intervals. And, of course, we have had running water for years in the house. Water is pumped up into a storage tank that is nestled in our large fig tree and then piped into our house from there. A forty-five-gallon drum enclosed with bricks serves as an oven for heating water when a fire is lit under it. We not only have cold running water, but also hot.

I almost forgot to mention that the only real convenience that we still lack out here is an indoor toilet. Yes, Simon Robinson put one inside when he filled in while we were on furlough in 1970, but it is not reliable due to the high water table in the area. So we still use the outdoor one which has stood the test through the years. Mind you, it also was a problem during the floods that I shared about in the last book, *To a Land He Showed Us.*

Our children have grown up here and love the bush. Colleen, like me, regrets having to leave our home. She has mentioned it often in the last while. Recently, the children and I climbed the second pyramidal hill to view the valley spreading out all around us. It was my last trip with all of them. I did go again with Kirk after that. This time we went up the south side of the third hill. No matter how often I have climbed these pyramid-shaped hills, I have enjoyed the view immensely each time.

I will miss the awakening call of the yellow-necked spurfowl. The sounds of the bush have always had an exhilarating effect on me. There is no tonic that can take its place. Even those creatures inside have a way of making you watchful. A spider in your pajamas or a gekko dropping on top of you from the ceiling while you are still rubbing the sleep out of your eyes does wonders for you! The nights were always safe—that is, if you stayed indoors. Wandering hyenas and prowling lions filled in as our guard dogs. Soon after our arrival a man-eating lion near here was killed by the Masai.

Our next home will be near Kisii in southwest Kenya. This will shorten our travelling time to visit the children at RVA on the long weekends. No more border crossings after this. There is one trip that we will always remember when returning home with the children at end of term. It was already midafternoon and we were still twenty-five miles away from the Tanzania border when a Masai kid herding cattle beside the road pitched a stone into our windscreen. It shattered on impact! I managed to stop the vehicle, in spite of bits of glass flying into my face, without driving off the road.

After checking that everyone was okay, I lit out after the kid, who already was running after realizing what he had done. I followed him into the tree line and caught up with him in the middle of the bush. What was I going to do with him? Beat him? No, I was going to take him to the police station that we had just passed at Kajiado. There they could decide whether his father will pay for a new windscreen. But that was not to be. The kid of about eight or nine started shrieking something in his language and clawing me with his free hand. He was also using his teeth, trying desperately to set himself free. I will have my hands full trying to drag him back to the vehicle.

I did not get far when several Masai appeared out of

nowhere brandishing spears . One was an older man, and I took him to be the boy's father. He had hurried over to deliver his son from his attacker, for surely this is what the kid had been screaming about. I tried to explain to the man what his son had done and that he could come and see for himself, but he appeared not to understand Swahili or English. I still had a vicelike grip on the kid's wrist and began to drag him along in the direction of the vehicle, which was yet out of sight.

The Masai were not going to put up with me any longer, and a couple of the *morani* (warriors) began jumping up and down and waving their spears. I knew then that they were working themselves up into a fighting mood. The kid was still babbling something while the father looked on knowing that soon his son would be free.

The third warrior now spoke to me in broken English: "Go; leave the boy."

I answered him, "I can't; he must come with me to the police."

The two *morani* were now in high gear; their chanting had gained in volume and pitch. I sensed danger. They were only waiting for the old man to give the signal. The warrior who had spoken in English now said, with an urgency in his voice, "Go! Now!"

I reluctantly released the boy and not any too soon, for they had begun to advance with their spears drawn. I backed off and they did not follow when they saw the boy was now free. I reached the vehicle after some minutes. I did not realize that I had gone that far into the bush! What if they had killed me? Would the family have found me? To make it worse, darkness was setting in. I finally came to my senses. The windscreen was not worth more than my life.

Needless to say, the family was happy to see me make an appearance. We drove home the rest of the way without a windscreen. It was cold. I wore my sunglasses, which made the night still darker, to keep the bits and pieces of glass that hung around the edges from flying into my eyes. Marion and the children stayed huddled over. It was a trip we will not forget! And I lived to write about it.

As I mentioned earlier, we will be moving to Kenya, living at Ibeno Mission. Doug Welch drove us out to see the place when we were in Nairobi several months ago. I finally consented to the move only after much advice from others and the missionary board. Their argument was that until the *Baba* (father) leaves his children, they will never really be on their own. African custom demands that children always respect their elders. And so, as long as I am around, the church leaders in Mbugwe and Uburunge will keep looking to me, the founder, for leadership.

No one will be replacing us immediately here at Kaiti. No one here to follow the tracks that we are leaving behind? It will take someone special who will agree to live in the bush, one who has a call from God for it. Roy and Magaline Hoops, who moved down from Kenya in 1971, are at Mirambo Mission. A year later the Farmers returned to Canada. They were replaced at Mbulu Mission by Bob and Jan Edwards from Kenya.

We completed the tabernacle at Kaiti Mission in time for our final assembly meeting. Bill Konstantopoulos, pastor of one of our supporting churches, was present at the dedication service. This was followed with our farewell service at Mirambo Mission in Uburunge and then, finally, the one here at Kaiti Mission. Marion and I sang "Rock of Ages" in Kimbugwe for the last time to our people. The Waburunge and the Wambugwe have showered us with so many gifts. The Wambugwe especially have always loaded us down with presents whenever we went on furlough. And they have outdone themselves again at this farewell. What love! The children, home from school this month, have gone with us to all of these functions.

It is August the twenty-fifth, 1974. Today, we are saying our final good-bye to those who since early morning have been gathering on our veranda. The vehicle and trailer are loaded and ready to go. There is no joy in my heart, but I manage to keep back the tears. Unknown to others, I have wept unashamedly on numerous occasions since the day I listened to what my head was saying and not my heart. Everyone is sad as we embrace one another. I end with a word of prayer.

We pull out of the yard at 10:30, passing between the two palm trees I had left standing when we first settled here. I glance back at the house we built out in the bush. There are now flowering shrubs and trees around it. I never dreamed I would ever leave it. They are back there waving, the people I have learned to love, maybe too much. We are leaving them behind. Will I meet any of them again? Then, I see them no more. There is only dust and our tracks. I do not look back again.

Chapter Twelve
The Wagusii

We leave Kaiti on August 26, spend the night in Arusha, and cross over into Kenya the following day. In Nairobi we shop, and it isn't until the day after, the twenty-ninth, that we reach our new home.

Ibeno Mission Station is resituated fourteen miles east of Kisii in the highlands of southwestern Kenya just east of Lake Victoria. The altitude here is 6,000 feet above sea level, much higher than what we were used to in Mbugwe where it is less than 3,000 feet above sea level. We have followed Jim and Dorothy Sharp, who have moved on to Kima Mission north of Kisumu. The house that we are living in was built by Simon and Mae Robinson, who have since retired.

The people in this area are the Wagusii, who belong to the Bantu-speaking group of Africa. To the west and to the northwest of the tribe live the Luo, who are Nilotic-speaking. The Kipsigis are their neighbours to the northeast and the Masai to the southeast. The Kuria, who are also Bantu-speaking and related to the Gusii tribe, live to the south along the Tanzania border. In the past the Wagusii have fought many wars with the Kipsigis and the Masai over cattle and land. There is no love lost between these tribes even to this present day.

The Gusii society is patrilineal, where the inheritance of property, including wives, passes from father to son. Women

116

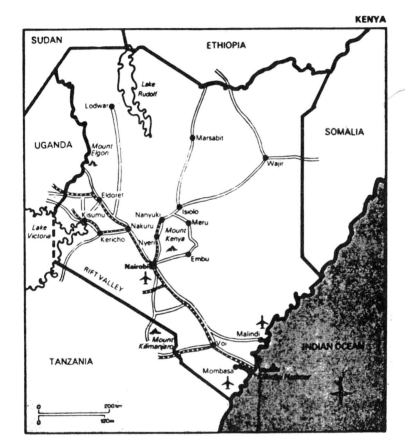

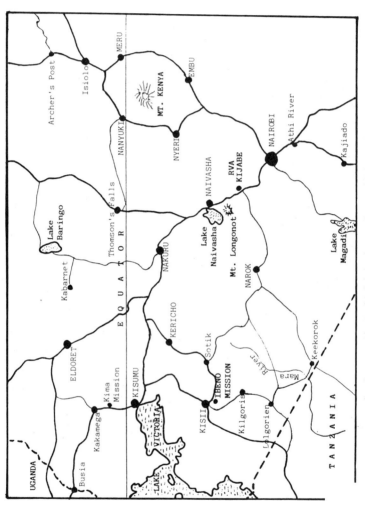

Our travels and ministry in southwest Kenya.

do not inherit anything from their men. Most Gusii families are very large because the men marry many wives. Co-wives will often compete with one another as to who produces the most children for their husband. Therefore, we find the women usually giving birth once every two years until they are too old to have any more.

We have discovered that the Wagusii practice the ancient custom of Levirate marriage. This is where the dead man's brother, or nearest male relative, is required to marry the widow and raise up children in the dead man's name. One reads of this custom being sanctioned by law in Deuteronomy 25:5–6, where the Israelite who has no male heir dies, his nearest relative must then marry the widow, and when the first son is born he becomes the heir to the dead husband.

It isn't long before we learn that several of the pastors and evangelists have Leviratical wives! No one has come to inform us about it, but we accidentally run across it in our travels to the churches here in Gusii. When discovered, to our surprise, they defend the custom vigorously! With no new land available and the population constantly increasing, plots of ground are becoming more valuable as they shrink in size. Therefore, they reason that the land of their deceased must, by all means, be kept in the family. The widow will not be allowed to remarry outside their kinship.

As logical as the practice may seem to be, the church leaders are removed from their posts. How many slipped through the net the Lord only knows! But suffice to say, this custom of Levirate marriages is brought out in the open, discussed, and acted upon according to the New Testament principles. The leaders in Gusii agree that this custom was only meant for the Israelites of that time and not for the Christians of today.

Most parents still want as many children as possible. They number in the double digits, often as high as eighteen! Afraid that some will die at an early age, these people have a large family to ensure the survival of their lineage. In doing so, the Wagusii reap countless other problems, where brother will eventually kill brother over a piece of land. Families that have many boys can no longer keep dividing the tiny plots of ground in order to give them a portion. The sons must now go elsewhere in search of employment. This they do after completing school.

All the hills in Gusii are covered with small plots of cultivation resembling that of a patch quilt. There is not a barren hill in sight no matter how steep it may be. This the most populated area in Kenya! Throngs of people are found moving along the roadside at all hours of the day. Children are everywhere, which Kirk, Mark, and I soon discover. They trail along behind us as we search for an out-of-the-way spot for hiking. We give up and return home, muttering about how wonderful the walks were at Kaiti, where we would have seen all kinds of wild game.

Marion enjoys her garden here at Ibeno. Where it was next to impossible to harvest any of the vegetables she planted at Kaiti because of poor soil, lack of rain, and wild animals, she now reaps the benefits of her labor. She is ecstatic over her new find! Every seed she plants not only comes up but also produces as well. Rain is plentiful here with no real dry season. Thus the Wagusii and Marion are able to plant the year round. How different from Mbugwe and Uburunge, where they eked out only one harvest annually, if there was rain.

Historically, the Wagusii have long believed in a supreme being called Engoro, who created the world and lives in the sky. With this background it was not difficult for the early missionaries to win converts to Christianity. Engoro is also invisible, omniscient, and just. He sends the rain or brings the drought, blesses with health or punishes with sickness. Even though Engoro controls man's fate, he does not interfere in his daily life. Any interference that may take place will come from their ancestral spirits.

I learn that the Wagusii do not worship the spirits of their ancestors. "They are all evil," I am told. But those who still fear them will sacrifice a sheep or goat in order to pacify them. At one time the people believed that ancestral spirits were Engoro's assistants and prayers had to be made through them. They performed certain tasks here on earth and dwelt on the distant escarpment. I need to add that these traditional religious practices still do flourish in parts of Gusii in spite of the advent of Christianity!

There are also witches in Gusii society, who operate to harm people and cause trouble for them. The *omorogi* (witch) is more often a woman than a man. Their actions are similar to those of the ancestral spirits, and it is often hard to distinguish between them, as they affect people in the same way. The main difference is that the *omorogi*'s intention is to disable or kill by magical means. She, or he, acquires the art of witchcraft from the parent, although it can be learned as well from others.

In Gusii belief, the witch runs around at night naked, carrying a light that is simply a pot with burning grass. An *omorogi* usually kills the victim with poison, but should you meet one at night it can be fatal. Killing a witch is encouraged, and thus the *omorogi* may find herself, or himself, being chased by youngsters with clubs. (This is the only weapon permitted for killing witches.) But the witches are noted to be fast runners, and rarely is one ever caught.

The poison that witches use is derived from leaves and roots. Parts of corpses taken from graves, hair, nail clippings, and excrement are also items that witches plant in their victims' houses in order to kill them. Hiring an *omoriori* (witch smeller) to search out the articles that have been placed there is the most popular method used by the Wagusii when be-witched.

Wagusii avoid eating in the house of a known witch. Even the educated agree that an *omorogi* will kill people by poisoning the food or drink. Most do not recognize that death is natural. It is always blamed on witchcraft. When a person has died, the first move is to consult a diviner. The *omoragori* (diviner) is one who diagnoses misfortunes and then prescribes remedies. He is able to communicate with the ancestral spirits for assistance and, therefore, able to detect witchcraft, interpret it, and identify the witch responsible for the death.

The next step now is for the household that has been bewitched to hire an *omonyamosira* (sorcerer) secretly to kill the poisoner or witch. Sorcerers are mysterious and fear-inspiring and possess magical powers. They are usually male and have received their training from outside Gusii, most likely from the Luo who are noted for their expertise in the art of sorcery. Where a death has occurred, the sorcerer commences to bury some of his medicine on top of the dead man's grave. The *omorogi* will die as soon as cracks appear on the grave!

I have been told that where no death has occurred in a bewitched home, the *omonyamosira* will bring some of his medicine, which may be only seeds, near the house. When the seeds crack open the witch will fall ill. But should the bewitched person know the identity of the *omorogi*, through the help of a diviner, the sorcerer will then scatter his medicine, which may be some ashes, on the path normally used by the witch. As soon as he touches it, the *omorogi* will die.

There is a procedure where the sorcerer will gain knowledge through using the greased stick, called *obomera* in the Kigusii language. This method is called upon not only in cases of witchcraft, but for theft as well. When someone stole several items from the office of our primary school on the mission station, the police were contacted. They failed to solve the case. Marion and I were away during the day, and so I do not know who it was that contacted the sorcerer to come and perform *obomera*. But this is what I was told after we returned from our trip to Nairobi.

The *omonyamosira* assembled the parents, teachers, and students in front of the school. Then he placed the greased stick on the ground and had them take turns in jumping over it. When I heard that our pastor took part in the activity I was thoroughly annoyed with him. But the end result was that one of the secondary school students tripped over the stick and consequently was charged by the sorcerer as being the thief. Strangely enough, the boy confessed that he was the one who stole the things!

We have discovered that witchcraft is still quite deep-rooted in Gusii society. In fact, all the way up the educated ladder! The following incident is an example of just such a case.

There is an empty lot situated at the fork where one road leads off left towards Kilgoris and the other continues on to Keumbu. One day I ask why the beginnings of a house on the piece of land are not being completed. In fact, each time I pass by no one is around. The answer is that the owner died in the process of building his house. It sounds mysterious, so I probe the man for more details.

An educated man from that area, who was working in Nairobi, upon seeing this empty lot claimed it and began erecting a house for himself, which he planned to live in upon retirement. But he soon ran into some problems. Someone claimed ownership of the land and demanded payment for it. A wrangle developed over who really owned it. Was the old man who appeared out of nowhere or was it the young, educated man? The local court failed to make a decision. In their last meeting together, the old man made this comment to the educated man: "You have only two more weeks to live."

Upon hearing this pronouncement of doom, the young man laughed and said, "I am an educated man I do not believe in witchcraft anymore!" He returned to his job in Nairobi, and what went through his mind no one knows. But exactly two weeks later, the young man dies. The report came out that he had died from a heart attack.

As I mentioned earlier, the lot is still empty. No further progress has taken place with the building since that fatal day a few years ago. How much did that old man have to do with the death? Was there witchcraft really involved? No one is pointing fingers. But the makings for it are there.

The medicine man (or woman) is highly respected in Gusii, and a clear distinction is made between him or her and the witch doctor. The one is loved and the other one hated. The *omonyamorigo* (medicine man) is trustworthy, upright, and able to discern people's needs. So say the Wagusii. He usually inherits his livelihood from his parents, although some declare that it was ancestral spirits who called him through dreams into this trade. The *omonyamorigo* is able to detect sorcery, purge witches, and remove curses. He is even able to control the spirits of the dead that may be restless and wishing to disturb the living.

Powder and juices are made from roots, leaves, seeds, and herbs, which he then uses to treat his patients. Bones and charcoal are ground up as well. He has love potions available for the women who want men to love them more, and there is help for the impotent men. Ailments such as diarrhoea, fever, pneumonia, and other kinds of aches and pains are cured by the *omonyamorigo* according to the Wagusii who purchase his medicines.

Marion had the opportunity twice to sample some *miti shamba*, the Swahili name given to any medicine concocted from trees and herbs. On the first occasion we were still in Tanzania and, while at Aimabu in Uburunge, Marion fell ill with a flu. She had a high temperature and diarrhoea. Salimu dropped in that day, and I mentioned to him that she was not well. He asked me then whether we had medicine for her illness. I had to answer him that we did not. Upon hearing this, he said that he would go and fetch some for her.

Salimu returned later in the day with something wrapped inside a piece of paper. Opening it up, we discovered small pieces of shredded bark. When asked to explain it, he said that the medicine came from a certain tree in the forest and that it would help Marion to get well quickly. All she had to do was steep one or two pieces in water for several minutes and then drink the liquid. At first we were reluctant to accept the *miti shamba,* but we gave in when we realized it came from God's creation. There were no rites connected with it from the medicine man. So Marion tried it, and the following day her fever had subsided and the diarrhoea was gone!

Her second experience with *miti shamba* occurred recently here in Gusii. Marion was suffering from what appeared to be laryngitis, which she had contracted several days earlier while we were visiting the children at Kijabe. A man who comes to our house each week to sell us pineapples noticed her condition. The following day he returned with some local medicine. "It is made from some plants that are found in Masailand," he told her. "I want you to try it for your sickness." Marion did and recovered rather quickly.

Had we prayed for her healing in both of these cases just mentioned? Yes, we had, and I believe God had His hand in the herbs of the field both times. It was not by chance that the cures showed up at our door. The Creator has a remedy for all the diseases that have befallen mankind, and we need to hunt for them! Why allow the medicine man in Africa to monopolize the trade? His usage of herbs of the field borderline divination too closely to be acceptable in Christian society.

Chapter Thirteen

The Lost Keys

Because the church has been in Gusiiland since the year 1948, we find the work quite advanced. There is not only a primary school in the mission compound, but a secondary school as well. It does not take long before I am asked to teach Christian education three times a week. I find it a challenge and quite enjoyable. The students are eager to learn, which makes it rewarding.

Marion immediately takes charge of the preschool clinic that Dorothy Sharp has been running at Ibeno. Each month 200 malnourished children, 50 per week, are provided with food that is donated by UNICEF. The organization also supplies the clinic with the scales and family planning materials. Many of the babies who are brought suffer from kwashiorkor, a disease resulting from a deficiency of protein in their diet. It is readily detected by their reddish or golden-colored hair and distended tummies.

The preschool clinic very quickly grows to 300 different children who are assisted monthly by Marion. She enlists the services of the nurses who work in our dispensary and maternity hospital on the mission. They immunize the babies and lecture the mothers on child care in their language. Marion teaches the women how to prepare and cook the food they are receiving and to make sure that the children who need it will get it.

One Wednesday, the day of the week that she always has the preschool clinic, Marion decides to have them all come in, all 300 mothers and their babies, for a class on family planning. She serves them bread and tea to close the day's activities. Each loaf is cut into three pieces and then handed to a woman with a cup of very sweet tea. Suddenly there is a ruckus at one table and Marion rushes over to check it out. Two ladies are standing up and flailing their arms about, often landing blows on each other!

Marion calms them down and discovers that one of the women had tried to take away someone else's bread and so a scuffle resulted. Marion takes her own piece of bread and then gives it to the one who was trying to steal from her neighbour. At seeing this, the rest of the women commence shaming the covetous woman. It was a good lesson for all, a lesson not soon forgotten—not to covet what belongs to someone else.

During another clinic, an all out-and-out fight does take place! As soon as the women arrive, they are given numbers and then form a queue. One latecomer pushes her way to the head of the line instead of waiting her turn. This upsets the rest of the ladies, and they begin shoving her to the rear of the queue. A fight ensues. Everyone on the compound is now involved! At this moment I am on top of a ladder, repairing the eaves trough on the maternity ward. I have the best seat on the station and witness the scrap from beginning to end. The ruckus has also brought the outpatients to their feet from where they were lounging in the shade.

Marion, who is inside weighing babies, marking cards, and giving out food, is summoned to come outside quickly. She rushes out and finds the two women on the ground trying to strangle each other. They stop fighting and get to their feet when ordered to do so. Marion then brings them all inside and resumes her clinic. When it is completed, she asks the women to discuss the incident that had just transpired outside.

Their decision is that the lady who wanted to push her way to the front should, for the next four weeks, be the last one in line! That should teach her to wait her turn.

In spite of the different problems that turn up at these clinics, Marion enjoys having them. Seeing children with discolored hair, lackluster eyes, and totally unresponsive at times change as mothers follow instructions brings her much satisfaction in what she is doing. She is always able to tell when the woman does not feed the baby but comes for the food only because the child does not improve. But if the woman follows instructions, the baby's hair gets black and curly again and the child begins to liven up.

There are three conventions that are held annually at Ibeno, one for the youth, one for the women, and then one for the general public. They are all well attended each time. It is a highlight to have Eliezer and Romonah come up from Tanzania to be the speakers at one of our youth conventions. Their ministry in teaching and preaching brings lasting results. It is nice to work together with them again, but the time to bid farewell comes all too soon.

We introduce a seminar for the pastors where we hold classes all day long, with a service in the evening. It takes them a while to get accustomed to sitting for long periods of time, but after a few days they do settle in. Solomon Sumbe, one of our evangelists in Tanzania, assists us with one seminar that goes for five days. It concludes with the Lord's Supper and a footwashing service, which is a first for most of the pastors.

Marion holds seminars with the women in their various districts. They may be as long as three days. The women come together to receive teachings pertaining to their needs. Marion usually takes along a nurse or midwife to assist her with the classes. When it is over, the women leave wiser in the Word and more informed concerning their well-being. After these outings, Marion returns home quite drained from all the speaking, which can last far into the night, or from singing until daybreak. She is very popular with them, and there is a scramble as to who will get to sleep beside her. This is so they can pump more information from the white woman who is not above sleeping on the floor with them inside the church.

There is one morning that Marion will always remember. After a few hours of sleep, she gets up and begins to roll up the mat that she has been sharing with the midwife from Ibeno. To their surprise, they discover a cobra! It crawled inside during the night seeking some warmth, and the place it chose was under Marion's mat. Mary, the midwife, quickly dispatches it with a stick. That was close! Either one could have been bitten by this very poisonous snake, which would have proven fatal, as the seminar is being held at Kenoria, in the remote area near Masailand.

Ever since our move to Kenya, Marion has had several bouts of hives. Tests reveal no allergies to food or things she uses or wears. The only thing left that may cause their sudden outbreaks is climatic. It is cooler and higher here in Gusii than back in Mbugwe. But she does not let hives interfere with her schedules. And so it is that she keeps her appointment with the women for a seminar at Tambacha. This time I do go along to assist her with the evening services, also to meet with the pastors and church leaders. Neely Kerich, a nurse at Kisii, accompanies us to teach the classes on health and family planning.

Because Marion honours her commitment, the Lord helps her out. The hives disappear altogether the following day! She is able to carry on and complete the seminar without any discomfort. Praise the Lord! Our nights during the seminar are spent on the floor of a house belonging to a teacher. He got it ready for his guests, Gusii style, by polishing the mud floor with fresh cow dung. Its strong smell is almost unbearable. How often we have come to a church for a Sunday service only to find the floor freshly plastered with cow dung. If it is still too wet, we have to be careful or we may slip and go for a slide!

A seminar that stands out above all the rest is one where Marion loses the key to our vehicle. This seminar is at Bomondo. She takes along Teresa, the nurse from our hospital; the pastor's wife; and James, the youth leader, to assist her with the classes, as it will be three days long. By the time their clothes, bedding, drinking water, and teaching material are packed inside, the vehicle is full. Then they are off. It is a forty-mile trip to their destination. I am left behind without a vehicle to get around. I will be walking to the service at Kabosi this Sunday.

As soon as Marion and her staff arrive, they are invited inside for tea. She accepts the offer and locks the vehicle so that no one can steal any of its contents. There are women present from six different churches. They have come with their bedding, mats, and some food. After tea, it is decided to hold the service earlier, as there is no moon until much later. Some of the women who live nearby wish to go home before dark.

Marion walks over to the Landcruiser to fetch her material for the service and discovers she does not have the keys! She goes through her pockets thoroughly but comes up empty. How can she get inside now? All their bedding, clothing, and teaching material is safely locked inside. Even her Bible, which she now needs for the service. She silently prays for the Lord to help her, and this verse of Scripture comes to mind: "Trust in the Lord with all thine heart and lean not onto thine own understanding. In all thy ways acknowledge Him and He shall direct your path" (Proverbs 3:52–6).

The women assist Marion, searching everywhere for the keys, even in the outhouse. But no one finds them. She tries the handles on the Landcruiser, but it's locked. Then she feels impressed to pound on the handle of the front door on the left side. As soon as she does, the knob inside pops up! "Praise the Lord!" she shouts. Now they are able to remove their belongings and start the service.

The two women who have come with Marion now speak up: "We were teasing our husbands that we are going on a safari [journey] with Mama and we are not coming back for a very long time. Maybe it will come true?"

She answers them, "No, God will help us get home."

After the service, there is food and fellowship. Then it is time to bunk down on the mud-and-cow-dung floor of the church. As Marion is spreading her blankets, she asks the Lord for some assurance that He will help them to get home. Reading her Bible, she comes across Hebrews 10:23: "Let us hold fast to the profession of our faith, without wavering for He is faithful that promised." She believes that the Lord will either help someone to find the keys, as she had put out a reward, or do it in another way to glorify Himself.

In the morning James, the youth leader, comes to her and offers to return to Ibeno Mission for my set of keys. "If I cut across country I can be back by tomorrow evening," he says.

She answers him, "No, James, God will help us to get home."

And so all day they hold their classes and Marion walks about as if she has the keys in her pocket. When someone asks, "Do you have the keys?" her answer is: "No, but God will help us get home." In spite of her raising the reward, the day wears on without anyone coming up with the lost keys. There are children searching for them everywhere.

By evening the devil is sitting on her shoulder and saying, *You are really going to look a fool tomorrow when the seminar ends and no keys!* Marion again turns to the Word for assurance and finds it in Romans 10:11: "Whosoever believeth on Him shall not be ashamed." Then a similar verse pops out at her in

Psalms 31:17: "Let me not be ashamed O Lord for I have called upon thee." Praise God! She goes to sleep that night knowing that He will see her through victoriously. And she sleeps well.

Sunday arrives, the last day of the seminar. After lunch they are to leave for home. James approaches Marion again about going for the extra set of keys. He may still be able to return with them by nightfall should there be transport available along the way. But her answer is still the same: "The Lord will get us home." They enter the church and commence with the service. The building is overflowing with people. Many are crowded around the windows as well. The news has gotten out that the white woman has lost the keys to her vehicle and is telling everyone that God will still get her home! Now they want to see how this will be done.

During the service the local pastor makes a last- minute plea that whoever has found the keys to return them now and receive a substantial reward. No one steps forward with them. The service ends and still no keys. The congregation is dismissed and Marion joins the ladies who attended the seminar in some food. When she comes out to go to the vehicle she discovers the congregation has not gone on home but is now assembled around the Landcruiser! They are awaiting the outcome of this saga.

Marion and the rest of her crew pack the things they had come with into the vehicle. She discovers there is a flat tire! What more can happen? This takes some time, as she has never changed one on a big vehicle. But she manages, with the help of several bystanders. This done, Marion lifts up the hood. She remembers it can be started by connecting certain wires. But which ones? There are too many of them to choose from. *Besides,* she thinks, *I may get an electrical shock which will not bring any glory to God.*

She drops the hood and climbs into the driver's seat. The time has now come to start the engine. Marion prays, *Lord, you said in Your word that I would not be ashamed if I trusted in You, and I am trusting totally in You.* All eyes are on her. Then, the thought comes to her: *Ask if anyone has keys.* This she does. Standing right beside her door, watching her every move, is a man who says he has a set of them. He produces them and adds that they are for the padlocks on the school. The man turns out to be the headmaster.

The ring contains an assortment of keys Marion commences to try to see if one will fit into the ignition. She is not disheartened when the first few fail but keeps on trying others. When the sixth key is tested, it falls into the ignition. She turns it, and the engine roars into action. The crowd is absolutely stunned! Marion leaps out of the vehicle, at the same time praising the Lord. She asks the people to gather around to offer up praise and thanks to God for the miracle He had just performed. They sing "To God Be the Glory" in Swahili, and then she offers up a prayer in which she thanks God for never making anyone ashamed when he or she trusts in Him.

Dark clouds are approaching, so Marion and her passengers need to leave the hills in a hurry. Borrowing the precious small key, with the promise to return it, she heads down the hill. All the preaching, teaching, singing, and praying has had its toll on Marion, and before she reaches home she loses her voice. Only a whisper remains. Not only is she not saying anything, but the rest are quiet as well. She enquires in a whisper what their problem is. Teresa replies, "I have never seen God answer prayer before. This weekend I have seen a miracle!"

They arrive home at 6:00 P.M., as Marion had promised those with her they would. She has Teresa relate the events of the weekend, as her own voice now utters only a faint whisper. I take the small key to test it on the vehicle myself. It will not be returned to the headmaster should it work again. I do not want him driving my Landcruiser away one day while it is parked in town. But no matter how much I try to start the motor, the key does not work! It had worked only for Marion in order to get her home. Truly, this was a miracle of God!

The headmaster receives his key back on our next trip to Bomondo. In the service Marion asks the congregation what they remember from her last visit. They reply, "To keep trusting the Lord to the very end!" Amen. Some lessons that God wishes to teach others often involve all the faith we as individuals can muster. We dare not fail when that happens. Marion did not, and God used her to teach others to trust Him as well.

Teresa, the nurse, when she saw the miracle began to believe Him for one in her own life. For seven years now of married life she had not given birth to a child. Her husband had beaten her on several occasions and is threatening to dismiss her for another woman. Teresa comes to us and asks for prayer that she will be able to conceive. A miracle takes place and she bears a child. Praise the Lord!

Our home at Ibeno Mission.

One of the conventions held outside the tabernacle.

The author and his family.

A shipment of the hymnbook *Nyimbo za Ibada*.

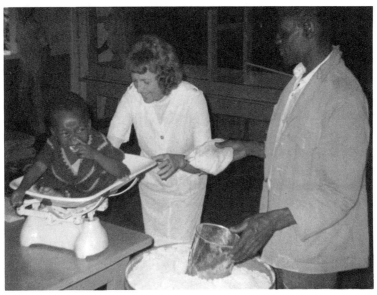

Marion busy with her preschool clinic.

Loading the vehicle for the children's return to RVA.

Rift Valley Academy at Kijabe.

With my sister Doreen near Maseno.

One of our churches in Gusii.

Where Marion discovered a snake under her mat.

With Rufus and the chief in Masailand.

Marion and some members from the church.

A Masai doing their traditional leaping.

The hill we climb to reach Ilchartiyani Church.

Away from the crowds, relaxing beside a hippo pool.

Mark celebrates his birthday while on safari.

Even Mom and Dad celebrate their anniversary in camp.

The warthog carrying tusks with a spread of over sixteen inches.

Colleen with her eland.

With my topi.

Kirk and his wildebeest.

Mark with his hartebeest.

Colleen and the buffalo she dropped with a single shot.

Kirk with his fine buffalo.

Mark and his impala.

With my prized Grevy zebra.

Colleen and her twelve-foot crocodile.

One of the crocodiles I bagged.

Kirk with his zebra.

Mark and his Thompson gazelle.

Baptizing converts in Masailand.

Marion teaching the Masai women.

One of the churches just erected in Masailand.

A goat given to me by the Masai.

Marion at a women's seminar in Gusii.

An old Gusii woman surrendering items used in divining.

Teaching Christian education in the secondary school at Ibeno.

Harambee Day for our new secondary school building.

Obokhano, the eight-string lyre of Gusiiland.

The monkeyskin hat and beaded skin cape given me by the Gusii.

Colleen excelling in sports at RVA.

Graduation Day!

Chapter Fourteen

The Stoning

We find the Wagusii very different from the Wambugwe and Waburunge. They are loud, while the people in Tanzania were soft-spoken and more mannerly. Since coming to Ibeno, we have had pastors and church leaders just walk straight into our house unannounced! Always at Kaiti the Wambugwe would announce themselves by saying *"Hodi?"* ("May I come near?") and then wait for your *"Karibu"* ("Welcome") before approaching your door. They would not enter your house until you came to the door and allowed them inside.

The Wagusii are noted to be quarrelsome. It does not take me long to find this out. In one of my first committee meetings with the church leaders, it gets so hot between some of them that I feel like crawling under the table. There was no diplomacy practiced at all. But I have met many who are friendly and most cooperative when planning the work of God in Gusiiland. Backbiting is extremely common, especially among the women. The feminine gender is much more easily provoked, and fistfights do erupt very quickly between them as seen in the previous chapter.

The youth are quite rowdy, particularly the boys. They are not one bit embarrassed to raise a ruckus outside the building while an evening service is being conducted inside. On several occasions they have even resorted to throwing stones onto the roof. We find this taking place upon our arrival at Ibeno

Mission, especially during our conventions. Placing a watchman outside to guard the building proves futile, as the rascals blended into the darkness too easily to be caught. I finally discuss the problem with the members of the local church after a Sunday service. I tell them they are responsible for their children's actions. This proves fruitful, for the hooliganism ceases.

During our years at Kaiti we never employed a watchman, as I mentioned before. There was no need for one, as the mission station was far from a city or town, where thieves normally hang out. It is situated in the bush, where wild carnivoras prowl at night. They kept us safe at night, how many times we never will know, from any thief who may have evil intentions. Moving here to Ibeno Station, we discover a fully employed night watchman. He has been with the mission for very many years and is now an old man. I find him sleeping at his job so many times that I finally give up, as I am told he cannot be fired.

We eventually hire a watchman for the days we are gone, as pineapples and vegetables in our garden turn up missing when we return. Logs are even stolen during our absence. They are from the eucalyptus trees we cut down for firewood during the cool season. There is a storeroom in the compound, and one night during a convention a couple of fellows try to break into it. Fortunately, the cooks hear them and the theft is thwarted. It takes place while Marion is speaking. She has to stop in her sermon until things have settled down and all has returned to normal.

I do catch a thief one evening stealing the lightbulb in the outdoor kitchen. On two previous occasions bulbs disappeared, but this time the culprit is caught in the act. He is still up near the rafters where he has climbed to remove the bulb. I grab his leg and pull him down. When asked what he was doing up there, he answers that he is catching birds! He denies taking the bulb, and yet when I search him I discover it in his pocket. When I learn that he is a boy attending secondary school, I report him to the headmaster. The boy receives the cane four times.

On one occasion I do set a young man free. He is brought to me bound up with cords and accused of being a thief. Some things have disappeared from the station recently, and this youngster is caught snooping around. It does look suspicious but there is no proof and so I ask them to release him. I probably save him from a severe beating from the police. His mother is very grateful and drops in with a *debi* (four-gallon tin) of millet. She gives it to us for a gift in appreciation for saving her son from going to prison.

They can deal quite severely with wrongdoers. What the man was guilty of no one really knows for sure, but he is found tied to a tree just across the marsh from here. He has been dead for three months! During Jomo Kenyatta's presidency, it was encouraged to stone a thief if he or she was in the act. Thereafter, it is not uncommon to see this enforced. One day in Nairobi as Marion is near the main post office, she hears a lady cry out, "Thief, thief!" Immediately those who see it happen are in hot pursuit of the thief, who is darting across the street. But he has no hope of escaping. There is now a crowd, and they seize him. Before a passing policeman arrives, the thief is dead, beaten beyond recognition!

While waiting in my vehicle, which is parked in front of some shops in Kisii, I witness a young man receiving a thorough beating from an irate gang. When I enquire as to what the problem is, I am informed that the man is a thief. Will they kill him? He is sitting on the sidewalk and desperately trying to protect his head from the vicious blows. What should I do? There is no policeman in sight. I reverse the vehicle and head for the police station. I finally convince the reluctant officer to accompany me to the scene. We find the gang still thrashing the shoplifter with their fists and sticks they have picked up somewhere. When the policeman orders them to leave, the gang readily disperses. The thief is jerked to his feet, which are unsteady, and then marched off to the station by the officer. Was I the only one around interested in saving the man from a further beating and maybe from death?

I find myself today in front of the garage here in Kisii waiting for the Landcruiser to get done. It has been here quite often since our move to Kenya. The rough miles we travelled with it while in Tanzania and now here are beginning to take their toll. Without it we would not be able to get around as we have. We thank the Lord for the four-wheel-drive vehicle.

While sitting on my haunches, I hear the crowd before I see it coming running down the alley that runs alongside the garage. There are only males in the group, which is getting larger as more are joining in. They are clamoring and shouting something, but I am unable to make out what it is. A short distance ahead of them is someone who, it appears to me, is trying to outrun them. He manages to cross the main road, not far from where I am, and enters the alley ahead of them. It is here that the noisy crowd catches up to him and the mad chase abruptly ends.

There is still much shouting from the crowd and there is a lot of frenzy in the air. What is this all about? What is happening down there? When it does not stop after some minutes, my curiosity gets the best of me and I begin to saunter towards the commotion. Before I can reach the throng, one of them detaches himself and comes towards me. I ask him what all the *kelele* (noise) is about, to which he replies, "It is all over."

I do not understand and ask him, "What is all over?"

He then explains that they have caught a thief and that they have just finished him off.

I am shocked! I can hardly believe my ears. I have sat by

and watched a man just get killed! As I turn to retrace my steps to the garage, I take another look at the yelling mob and spot a movement through the maze of legs. I spring into action and rush over to the wall of people. There must now be close to 100 in this crowd. By elbowing my way, I reach the scene of action. There on the ground at my feet lies a man, his face covered with blood and the corner of his head smashed in.

He is still alive, just barely, and his clothes have nearly all been ripped off. Because there is still life in him, those close by keep pelting him with stones. I find myself standing beside a tall man who is in the process of lifting a good-sized rock above his head. That rock if it lands on his head will surely put the thief out of his misery. I find myself grabbing the man's hand. The surprise move causes him to drop it. It lands on his own feet! He screams out loud and turns to see who it is that stopped him from delivering the coup de grace.

The man stares at me and then begins shouting, "Why have you interfered?" I boldly tell him and the rest, who are now staring at me, not believing what they are seeing, that they are breaking the law just as much as the one they are stoning did. The reply is that they have the right to stone a thief, as the president has given a decree that says thieves can be stoned to death. I go on to say that they have the law of the land that takes care of such matters and they should not be guilty of spilling blood.

I go on to say much more, reasoning with them until tempers begin to cool. During the whole discourse, the thief has been listening as well, and now he reaches up to grab my hand. He believes now I may be able to save his life after all. I assist him to his feet and then start leading him through the mob. Will they let me pass safely? Those near enough swipe at him with their fists, many of them landing. I narrowly miss getting hit myself. Only the Lord is protecting me in this rescue venture, foolhardy as it may be!

It takes some time to break through the murmuring crowd, but I manage it, unscathed at that. But if I thought that they will now leave us to ourselves, I am mistaken, for they continue to move along with us down Main Street. No one has come to my aid. It is going to be a long walk to the police station, three and a half blocks away. The mob is still hostile, and anything can happen. I look at the man I am leading along, and it is hard to see what he really looks like. His face is badly cut up and bloody.

As we move past a filling station, one of the attendants runs towards us wielding a long one-inch metal pipe. When he is near us he swings it at the thief's head. It would have connected had I not jerked him aside in the nick of time. Others keep trying to hit him with stones. How they miss me is a miracle. I ask the thief what it was he had stolen. He replies that it was five shillings from a woman who was about to board a bus. Five shillings! That is less than a dollar. I then ask him whether his life is not worth more than that. Had they killed him back there, that is all he would have been worth. They may yet before we reach the police station!

I am sure as I lead the thief down Main Street there are many who see us from the safety of their premises. Do they come forth to assist me? No, they do not! And so for two blocks I continue to stick close to the injured and bleeding man, doing all I can to protect him from his attackers, who are out to kill him because he stole five shillings from a woman. The thief does not attempt to escape, as he has seen that any chance he has of surviving is to stick with me.

We are nearing the corner where we must turn to reach the police station, a block and a half up the hill. Where are they anyway? Surely, one of them must be around somewhere who has heard the clamor or seen the mob coming up Main Street? But no policeman shows his face. When you are in need of one, he is not around. The temper of the crowd is lessening; their flailings have turned to insults. The crowd is thinning out as well. Lord, help me make it to the police station.

A landrover carrying government license plates pulls up alongside of us just as we reach the corner. It stops and the man inside asks me what the problem is. I explain and he agrees to assist me in taking the thief to the police. He dismisses the crowd and we load the thief into the vehicle. Then it is off to the police station, where he is turned over to the officer in charge at the time. I thank the man with the Landrover and he is off before I have a chance to ask him his name.

The police officer opens a docket on the man I have just brought in, who is about ready to drop from the severe beating he has received and all the blood he has lost. When done with the report, the officer says to the thief, "You have this *Mzungu* to thank for still being alive!" Then he is whisked away in a police vehicle to the hospital for treatment. Should he survive all the bodily bruises and cracked skull, he will be charged for the theft. But I believe he has already paid more than enough for the crime.

Finally, I am able to relax. As the shock of the whole episode wears off, my knees begin to buckle and I have to hang onto the counter for support. I suddenly realize what I had done! I could easily have been killed in the incident. The mob was out for blood. When I first entered the fray, the ones beating the thief turned into animals. Remembering all this sends a chill up my spine. It is only with the help of the Lord that I survived this highly dangerous situation, and I might add for the thief as well. It could have ended entirely different had it not been for Him!

Chapter Fifteen
Female Circumcision

We are rather surprised to find that female circumcision is still in existence here in Gusiiland after decades of Christianity! We found it practiced wherever we went in Tanzania and now again here in southwestern Kenya. When will this female mutilation cease?

Nowhere in the Bible do we read of it being practiced. Circumcision was performed only on males, and that on the eighth day after their birth (Genesis 17:10–14). It involved the cutting off of the foreskin, a rite instituted by God as a sign of the covenant made between Him and Abraham. This custom was practiced from then on and is still observed in Israel today. However, Christians in the early Church refused to force the Gentiles to be circumcised (Acts 15:1–11; Galatians 5:1–6). It is the teachings of Jesus and His followers that we adhere to and follow today.

Shortly after our move to Ibeno Mission, the circumcision ceremonies commenced. They occur annually during the months of October, November, and December, with the girls preceding the boys in their initiation. It is early December when Marion and I are invited to attend one nearby. Just previous to this, we had been hearing the singing and ululating of the women as they passed by the station each morning with the girls. We fail to attend that one, but the following morning, after being awakened by loud trilling, I go to investigate and walk in on a circumcision ceremony taking place right here in the mission compound!

The small group is gathered on the far end of the primary schoolyard near the line of eucalyptus trees. It is quite cool and a heavy fog is lying quite close to the ground. There are six very young girls, around eight years of age, awaiting the operator to proceed with the clitoridectomy. Marion has done some research on female circumcision, and I will now share from her paper on a rite that is still practiced in the many tribes of East Africa today.

Whereas circumcision in boys may have begun as a religious rite, eventually recognized as an act of hygiene, circumcision in girl does not fall under either of these. It is primarily a tribal custom that African society can surely do without! We have discovered that the age limits for those qualifying to participate in the rite can vary between tribes. For instance, in Gusii the girls are quite young, around eight years of age, while in Mbugwe they are older, around twelve. But in Masailand, the rite is performed in their early teens. In fact, there was one who was at least sixteen during a female circumcision ceremony we attended while in Tanzania.

The site of the initiation ceremony for girls may vary as well between tribes. In Mbugwe they gather inside a hut, the Masai assemble at the entrance, and in Gusiiland they gather outside near a rock or tree. The operation is the same, though, and the one executing it will be an elderly woman who has done this for years. Much singing, dancing, and ululating has already taken place by the women as they make their way to the place of circumcision. Now they crowd around and witness the initiation that is ready to commence. While men are outlawed from attending in Mbugwe and Gusii, they may in Masailand. That is why I was able to be at one. (Marion and Kirk were with me that day.)

The girl to be operated on is seated on a stool. A woman

behind puts her arms around the girl to hold her firmly. (In Gusii, where the girl is yet so young, she may be seated on the knees of a woman who holds the girl's hands over her eyes so that she does not see what is happening.) The operator squats in front of the girl and applies white flour on the genital area. Without anything to deaden or lessen the pain, the woman swiftly cuts off the head of the clitoris with a razor blade or knife. As soon as the piece of flesh drops to the ground, the crowd of gathered women ululate, sing, and dance.

During the whole exercise, the girl is encouraged not to make a sound. She is highly praised for her bravery should she succeed. But if she fails, she is known as a coward who has brought shame to her family and will carry this stigma the rest of her life.

During childhood, she is not pampered and cuddled when hurt. So, slowly she gets hardened to the fact that it is no use making a fuss over pain. She is also taught to be passive whenever pain is inflicted. This is to prepare her for initiation day so that she will be able to go through the operation as though nothing is hurting.

After the clitoridectomy, she is led aside to bleed and to wait for the rest of the girls to be circumcised. When all of them have been operated on, the women commence escorting the girls back to their respective homes where food awaits them. Along the way, under the hot sun, obscene songs are being sung. The procession moves along slowly as the girls find it difficult walking, often stopping to rest beside the road under some shade. When they finally arrive, the circumcised are in such misery that food offered them is refused.

I need to mention at this time, before going further, that in Masailand when the clitoridectomy is complete on all the girls, they then line up, with blood streaming down their legs, in front of a row of young men seeking mates. Each girl now takes turn identifying the one she wishes to marry her, as she is of age. She walks up to him and either takes his spear or touches it. A shout of glee rises up from those assembled. The men failing to be chosen react with a lot of feeling, whether real or fake, and they may go into fits! Those picked, will immediately produce several cows, as if prearranged, for the father of the girl as a down payment for their engagement.

The songs sung after the initiation ceremony are coarse and lewd. Their words are concerned mainly with some aspect of sexual intercourse. As they dance and sing, there is much play fighting, all centering around intercourse, with women even putting their arms around each other and feigning the act. The circumcised are reminded that they are now too big to be embarrassed or inhibited. More obscene songs are sung as women move their hips suggestively.

During the leading-in ceremony, the women surround the girl as they lead her into the house. The men must not see her. (Women in Mbugwe hold a piece of cloth over the girl, canopy-style, in order to conceal her.) The father plays a minor role in the whole affair and cannot sleep in the house until the girl's one month of seclusion is finished. The mother provides plenty of food, as this is believed to assist in the healing of the wound. There are instances where several initiated girls will come together in the house of one of the mothers for the month-long seclusion.

Although the girl may only be eight years old, as in Gusii, she now is introduced to matters of courtship, marriage, birth, and family life. An instructor who is not the mother comes to teach the girl during her time of seclusion. Instructions will include personal cleanliness and how she should behave as a newly circumcised girl. Girls who have been initiated pre-viously come to visit her and share their sex adventures with her. Boys may, at this time, steal inside and have intercourse with these older girls.

A month later, another ritual takes the girl, or girls, out

of seclusion. She is smeared with a red and/or white mixture on parts of her body. A piece of cloth is wrapped around the lower part of her body, and beads given by relatives complete her attire. Boys who were circumcised during this time come out of seclusion all decorated and painted to join the girls in the coming-out ceremony, which is a large dance affecting the entire community. There are play fights and much feasting throughout the day. It closes with much drinking of their native beer.

After the period of seclusion, the life of each girl is now expected to be that of an adult. She now cleans the house, cooks food, and works in the garden with her mother. The girl is now interested in wearing pretty clothes and spends much of her time visiting the girls who were circumcised along with her. They eventually end up in public places in order to be seen by boys.

I need to point out that there have been cases of girls bleeding to death after circumcision. In one region of Tanzania seventeen girls, after being circumcised, bled to death in a single year. (When it was brought to their attention, the government issued a statement making female circumcision illegal in 1970.) Here in Gusii, a man came to me one evening asking me to take his daughter to the hospital in Kisii, as she was still bleeding after her circumcision that morning! There have been other cases.

Since the operator knows nothing about blood vessels, if she cuts too deep and severs them, there is a danger of the girl bleeding to death, as the woman does nothing to curb the flow. The danger is compounded as the initiation is done miles from any hospital. Infection is a possibility, as the instrument used to perform the operation on all the girls is not sterilized. Neither are the hands of the operator, who is dressed in her usual garb. The risk of spreading a disease is also likely, as the knife is simply wiped with a dirty rag. And then recuperating, during the month-long seclusion period, in a hut where livestock is kept greatly increases the danger of the girl's wound getting infected.

Because of the operator's ignorance of anatomy and using an unsterilized instrument, the girl can expect problems to develop not only during or soon after circumcision, but later on in life as well. When the clitoris is sliced off, tissues are broken around the urethra and the muscle that controls the release of urine is severed. She now will have difficulty in controlling the urine and will dribble. If the teacher at school does not allow the girl to go and attend to herself, she suffers the embarrassment of urinating right where she sits.

Due to the lack of control in this gland, the female section at a church service will be quite active. Reprimanding them does not help. I soon learned that in Mbugwe and Uburunge. If we did not want puddles on the floor, they were allowed to wander in and out at will. Rather a nuisance! There is also an increased chance of bladder infection because the urinary canal is now exposed. Proper personal hygiene is a necessity if they are to avoid any further discomfort.

The removal of the clitoris takes away feelings of sexual excitement and the reaching of a climax. Therefore, a lot of sexual looseness will take place in women of the tribes that practice clitoridectomy. She keeps thinking that the next man will give her the excitement and satisfaction she is craving. This constant seeking increases the chance of her contracting a venereal disease. We found the rate of VD very high in Mbugwe when we started there. And no wonder, when at *pombe* (native beer) parties young women each will lie with as many men as a dozen seeking some sort of fulfillment. Women drift from men to men, never staying for long with any of them. One woman we know has already lived with twenty different men! I am sure that most of the blame for it can be directed towards this pointless practice of female circumcision.

When a girl has been circumcised, the area that has been cut forms a hard scar tissue that will affect the mother at childbirth. During her first delivery this scar that is stiff will not stretch, thus preventing the baby's exit unless incisions are made. If she delivers at home and the scar tissue does not stretch, the mother and baby could die because no one knows what to do. Should the scar tear from the mother pushing the child, there is excessive bleeding due to so many blood vessels being broken. The damaged tissues will take a long time to heal, increasing the chances of infection, which can result in death.

Now, with all these problems facing her, why must a girl still be circumcised? I have asked this question countless times. The simplest answer they give is: "It is our custom." Traditions and customs are firmly woven into their society. It never occurs to anyone to question them. Thus, circumcision is still practiced because their ancestors did it and so they must do it, too.

In some tribes, female circumcision serves as a school in which the initiate is taught her role in society. The cutting of the sex organ symbolizes the break from the unproductive state to one of production. She leaves behind the status of being a "little girl" and commences to do women's work. As long as she remains uncircumcised she cannot get married and raise a family.

For fear of being ostracized by her age group in the village, she naturally will ask to be circumcised. If they are all done in that year and she is not, the girl will be excluded from their social functions. Thus she is pressured into joining the group that is being initiated so that they can all be together. Every girl wants to be the object of attention by circumcised boys and not by her own age group.

Parents do insist that their daughter be circumcised so that she can become marriageable. They believe an uncircumcised girl will not be sought after for marriage but will be left on the shelf, as only the circumcised are eligible because of their acquired knowledge, which is not accessible to the uninitiated. Where parents decide that a daughter should not be circumcised because they are Christians, the grandmother will take her to have the operation performed while they are away!

Today in East Africa, changes are gradually taking place. Certain traditions and customs such as tattooing the body, piercing the upper lip, and scarring the face are disappearing as a result of education and Christianity. The Wambugwe, who practiced facial scarification, have all but left it. This is partly because more girls attend school today and the government is discouraging the practice. Also, because missionaries have brought the teachings of Christ into their lives. Other tribes have completely left circumcision as a rite that initiates a child into adulthood and have accepted other rites to commemorate this occasion.

Chapter Sixteen

A Dream Fulfilled

Besides working with the Wagusii, we also have the opportunity to share the gospel with the Masai. We lived beside them in Tanzania and got acquainted with many of their ways. Our experiences with them are recorded in the previous book, *To a Land He Showed Us,* in chapter 12. I will, therefore, not elaborate on their life-style, customs, and beliefs, as those here in southern Kenya are quite similar to those in Tanzania. The only difference we find is that some of them here have taken up homesteads and are living in semipermanent structures.

There are three places of worship that have been started among the Masai near the Gusii border. Our first visit is at Olereko, where they have just erected a church building. James Chimbalambala from Tanzania, who is attending KTC (Kima Theological College) here in Kenya, is with us on this trip to the Masai. While in someone's house, I drink milk that is offered to me in a gourd. The charcoal taste is not too strong, and the stuff is palatable. I drank it often while calling upon the Masai in Tanzania. I did not think that I would ever have the opportunity again so soon to be in such close fellowship with them. A dream fulfilled!

Nearly 200 are present in the service. It is incredible to see so many of them worshipping the Lord at the same time! This we failed to see during our years in Tanzania. Marion and I are blessed as we watch them sing and take part in the service.

There are five children dedicated after the sermon, and promptly one of them is named Stanley and another one Hoffmani. I am off to a flying start!

On our way back to Ibeno, we swing around Kilgoris and down to the Migori River, where we run across elephant tracks. Topi, warthogs, impala, baboons, and ostriches are spotted as we travel along. Masai do not hunt wild animals as such; therefore, game is plentiful in their territory. In Gusiiland the animals have all been poached out and the land cultivated. Any good hunting left in Kenya is to be found in Masailand, which covers quite a large area.

The church at Ilchartiyani is on top of a hill three and a half miles north of Kilgoris. We are thankful for our four-wheel-drive Landcruiser, which we brought with us from Kaiti. Without it we would not have made it. (The altitude at this point is 6,900 feet.) There is hail when it rains this afternoon. We hold two services, one of them after dark. Our light comes from a little can containing kerosene that has a wick in it made out of string.

Because I forget the pegs and poles to our tent, we now have to sleep on the floor in one of their huts. It is after ten tonight before Marion and I roll up in our sleeping bags and call it a day. But our sleep is interrupted throughout the night by a barking dog. The Landcruiser must have disturbed him. As dawn approaches, a hen, which we had not noticed when we retired, gets up out of her nest and clambers over top of us to disappear into the next room. When a goat begins to bleat almost at our elbow, we decide to rise and shine.

Before we leave Masailand, there is more preaching and teaching. Marion takes time with the women, who are more teachable here than their kin back in Tanzania. There are sick to be prayed for, plus those who are oppressed by evil spirits. One of them explains how at night spirits appear to him in dreams and, at times, even awaken him. We pray for him and exhort him to take command over them in the name of Jesus. He must not allow them to interfere in his life again. This he does, and when we see him again, on our next visit, he has had no further recurrences.

The first baptismal service in Masailand is held near Olereko in a tributary to the Migori River. The water is very cold. There are twenty of them who follow Christ in this ordinance. Rufus Akhonya, who is the evangelist to the Masai, assists me in the water. The Lord's Supper, the first here as well, is served after the service in the church. It is observed again at Ilchartiyani. We discover the water in the nearby stream here is only a foot deep, so we postpone the baptism for our next trip.

We spend more and more time with the Masai. Rufus receives a bicycle so that he can cover a larger area. He loves walking and does not find it difficult to roam the hills in search of souls. The Masai love him and have accepted him into their midst. This is not readily done by this tribe to any outsider. Anyone from Gusii is not welcome, but since Rufus comes from Luya, beyond the Luo tribe, there is no enmity between them. He and I are the same age and we share the same goal—to see the work expand in Masailand.

This it does! Had we stayed longer we would have planted churches all the way to Narok. We are on the edge of the Rift Valley when we start one at Marrti. right beside the Mara River, near the Kipsigis border. The chief is with me on this trip. To reach the village we cross on a long, narrow footbridge that hangs over the river. It swings back and forth as we slowly traverse the span, hanging onto the railing all the way. The view below is breathtaking!

I am excited about the new church that we begin at Keyani. Of all the places, this one reminds me the most of the Masai near Kaiti. They live on cattle entirely and their window-less houses are built of mud-and-wattle, plastered with cow dung. The men's dress is a simple cloth that hangs from one shoulder, where it is tied in a knot. Women ornament themselves with coiled wire and beads around their necks. From their earlobes hang spirals of wire and flat leather straps that are beaded. Not one of them wears a European dress, only a cloth that she wraps around herself under the armpits.

The first time I go to Keyani, I fail to reach the spot where the church is to be built with my vehicle. The terrain is very rough and rocky, covered in thorns and brush. I end up walking the remaining two or three miles. The men want to hear what I have come to tell them, and so we meet for a service. It ends with prayer and an invitation to the assistant chief's house for food. The whole visit is a wonderful experience for me. I walk away with a leg of goat meat that the assistant chief gives me for Marion, who did not accompany me on this trip.

A way is eventually found to Keyani so that I am able to drive up to the site where the church is built. There are over 100 present for the service. Marion is along this time. She meets the women and has a class with them. They are all decked out in their finery! The *wazee* (old men) meet with me again. Our love for one another is mutual. It is great to just sit around and talk with them. Of course, Rufus is at my side. We eat and drink several times before it is time to come away from this quiet and simple spot in Masailand.

A day at Keyani that highlights them all is in April 1976. The whole family is with me on this trip. School is out for the month, and the children are with their mom and dad. Due to the recent rains, the road to the church is quite muddy, but we make it. In the first service we dedicate the church building. Then we walk down to a beautiful shady spot on the banks of the Migori River. There I baptize forty-six Masai and Mark, our son. The women who enter the water with hair neatly done up in red ochre mixed with cow manure soon discover their makeup dripping down their faces after immersion! I am sure they did not know this would happen.

After baptism we all return to the church and hold the Easter service, followed by the Lord's Supper. I also pray for the children who are being dedicated to the Lord. It has been a rewarding day! Before we can leave, though, we must help them eat some of the food that has been prepared for this special occasion in the life of the Masai.

New churches continue to spring up in Masailand. Most of them are in hard-to-reach places. The one at Osongoroi is situated in a village between some treeless hills beyond Ilchartiyani. I cannot reach the place with my vehicle. The Landcruiser must be parked at Poroko Village, and then the rest of the way I use my feet. Rufus leads the way. First we must climb the steep incline to Ilchartiyani. Then we wind our way between the hills until we reach Osongoroi. We have a service under a tree with those who have gathered and pray over the plot where the church will be built. Before we can leave, the ex-chief invites us in to eat with him. This we do.

When the church has been erected I return to dedicate it to the Lord. I must again tramp the nearly ten miles on foot to get there. About one hundred are present for the service. We pray for those seeking the Lord and for the children who are being dedicated by their parents. Again we eat at the ex-chief's house. This time I learn that he has five wives. Polygamy is keeping many of the older men from taking leading roles in the church. Our hope lies with the young men. There are some attending KTC currently, preparing for the ministry.

Kilgoris is the district headquarters for the Masai living on the escarpment above the Rift Valley. We make efforts to plant a church in this town. We visit the officials and a plot is granted. Plans are under way to build a dispensary here as well. My sister Doreen donates money towards the building of this church, and soon the making of cement blocks are under way which I inspect on my last trip to Kilgoris. I am again treated, before I depart, to drinking typical Masai milk with the charcoal flavor to it.

The tenth church among the Masai is planted at Angata, less than a mile from the Tanzania border. When we confer with the local chief, he gives us permission to build the church. The site we choose is near the hill Ol Doinyo Narok. I provide the *bati* (metal sheets) for the roof when the building gets under way. Cattle raids still take place along the border between the Masai on both sides. Before I leave, I take another look across to the other side and wish I had more time here in order to start planting churches among the Masai in Tanzania.

Megwarra, one of the three churches that had been started before our arrival, is finally making some progress. We had found it struggling to keep services going. There was a wedding scheduled to take place the day of my first visit, but the concerned party did not make an appearance. We learned later that the dowry or bride price had not been settled yet. The wedding finally does take place ten months later. It is the first Christian wedding in the area.

The baptismal that had been cancelled earlier at Ilchartiyani takes place, and I baptize twenty-eight in the Poroko River. Other baptisms follow as the church keeps growing numerically and spiritually due to the weekend seminars we hold here. Whenever Marion is with me she is sure to teach the women. The climb up the sheer hillside is quite strenuous for her. Another boy is named Hoffmani at a child dedication service. But this is not to be the last one with that name.

Our next trip to Ilchartiyani, I drive up to the church. Not only is it steep, but the vehicle leans to one side quite a lot in several places as we hug the side of the hill—one of the reasons I prefer leaving the vehicle at Poroko Village, where we now have a church, and climbing up the hill, however steep it may be. During this trip we again sleep on the floor. This time it is in the pastor's house. We have remembered to bring along our sponge mattress.

An hour after we bunk down, a stranger appears with the message that a woman is having problems with her afterbirth. Can my wife come quickly to assist this lady in distress? Marion packs a few things that she usually brings along for emergencies into a bag, and we light out after the bearer of bad tidings, the pastor at our heels. It is eleven o'clock and pitch-dark outside. I have my torch along to lighten up the way some, as we do not know where we are going, except the Masai who is leading us. He probably knows the way like the back of his hand, for he came this way in total darkness.

The path winds up and down, back and forth, for about two miles before we reach our destination. And not any too soon, because we are beginning to wonder if this is for real. The only light inside the one-room hut is coming from the live coals in the fireplace where they do their cooking. There are three women sitting on the floor and one lying on a cowskin. My torch reveals a baby near its mother. In fact, it is still attached to the placenta. The baby is quite cold, but still alive, and has been lying this way since its birth five hours earlier!

Marion calls for water to be heated so that the baby can be warmed up in it. She has brought along disinfectant, which is now used for the cutting of the cord. The mother has an inverted womb, which Marion now proceeds to push back inside. She has never seen anything like this before, but the Lord impresses her to do it this way. When done, she tells the mother to lie on her back for the next three days without getting up and moving about. This is to prevent the womb from inverting again.

The infant is bathed in the warm water and begins to show

168

some life immediately. The thankful woman asks us our name. The baby, a boy, is promptly named Hoffmani. The Masai who led us here now returns us safely to our place of rest. It is two o'clock. We soon are nested under our sheets and fast asleep. The walk and night air did us good. Before we leave Ilchartiyani two days later, the husband brings us the news that his wife is doing fine and so is little Hoffmani and expresses his gratitude by presented us with a rooster as a gift. When Marion checks at the hospital in Kilgoris to see whether she did the right thing, the doctor assured her that he would have done the same thing.

Our farewell is held at Olereko, the first church to be opened in Masailand. We have come here often. During those two years I have baptized many in the cold stream nearby. It always amazed me why the water in this particular stream was so cold. A child here has been named after Marion at one of our dedication services. How many bear our name among the Masai we do not know, and probably never will. But there are enough of them around to keep a memory of us alive for some time.

We receive typical Masai gifts. On an earlier trip, Gideon, in whose house we have slept on several occasions and where I drank some of the best milk I have tasted in Masailand, as it had been stored inside a hole dug in the floor of their hut for coolness, gave me his walking stick and Marion his beaded belt. Then at Ilchartiyani, the church presented me with a fly whisk made out of a cow's tail and Marion received a beaded wristband. Here at our farewell in Olereko, Marion receives a nice beaded necklace, which the Masai women wear, and I am given a real live goat! We manage to cart him home in one piece.

As I leave Masailand for the last time, I come across a massive buffalo standing near the road. He is alone and carries a good set of horns. I stop the vehicle and he allows me to look him over for several minutes before he decides I have had enough and lumbers away. But before the bull reaches some covering he stops, turns his head, and glances back at me. How does he know I am not carrying a gun? I bid him farewell and we go our separate ways.

I need to mention before I close this chapter that the enmity between the Masai and the Gusii tribe has lessened during the past year. There is still the odd scrimmage that takes place along the border, but not as it was only a few years ago when Masai warriors raided Gusii cattle deep inside Gusiiland. Too often lives were lost as well.

The day finally arrives when I meet with representatives from both sides and discuss building a church on the border at Nyabitunwa, the major crossing point between Kisii and Kilgoris. The residents of the village are from both tribes, with the Wagusii living on one side of the road, which is the border, and the Masai on the other side. As a result of the meeting the church does get built, right beside the road on the Masai side, in time before our departure. It stands as a reminder of the peace that Christ brought about between two tribes that were once enemies.

I have found working with the Masai a dream come true. While in Tanzania, I was unable to give them more of my time, as the gospel spread more readily in Mbugwe and in Uburunge. And so it has taken until our move to Kenya before my dream to plant churches in Masailand is fulfilled. I can now leave with satisfaction of having seen men and women of the Masai tribe accept Christ into their hearts and then actually live for Him.

Chapter Seventeen

Away from the Crowds

Marion and I try to give our children quality time whenever we are together, whether it is during their holidays or on long weekends. All too soon the day will arrive when one by one they will leave the nest. And so we take advantage of each opportunity to travel together and visit different parts of Kenya. All of us are keen on camping, which is easier on the pocketbook. Why do we leave the comforts of home? Why suffer thirst when we can drink cool water from the fridge? Are we daffy to bump over scorching plains hours on end? The answer simply is our thirst for adventure, the joy of being in the outdoors, entering as yet unknown to us territory that we want to discover.

This does not mean we do not spend time at home with our children. There are services and conventions that they attend with us. Colleen loves to assist her mother in the preschool clinic. Whenever Marion is away at a seminar, they will surprise her by doing all her work, including washing the clothes. I used to play games with them while still at Kaiti, but it is rare indeed that I find time to do it here at Ibeno. There are days we have company all day long, with visitors knocking at the front and back doors at the same time! They start coming at 6:30 A.M. and carry on until 9:30 P.M. There is no time for anything else but talk and listening to his or her *shida* (problem). I retire feeling guilty that the children have been neglected.

Thus it is that we draw away from the crowds to a quiet place in order to have time for one another. So you will notice in this chapter, and the next, many of our outings are spent in hunting. The boys and Colleen continue to fill my game licenses as we venture farther afield. Any meat that we cannot handle we drop off at their school, where it is gladly received. Many precious memories are recorded during these times out in the untamed.

My sister Doreen flies out to visit us in October 1975. Colleen is with us to meet her at the Nairobi airport. (I had quite a time getting permission for Colleen, just like trying to get someone out of the pen!) Doreen, who has been a steady supporter of the work, is my first relative to visit us in Africa. At the RVA guest house, there is a lot of excitement in the evening when she unpacks her luggage and hands out gifts to all of us. Better than a birthday or Christmas! The following morning Marion and I take Doreen down to Kaiti Mission, leaving the children at school.

Eliezer, Romonah, and Angelina are glad to see us again and to meet Doreen. It is good to be home. We walk to the dry riverbed and notice that elephants had come to drink at the waterhole last night. Like old times! Their tracks are visible everywhere on the sand. A Mangati *boma* is nearby, and we walk Doreen over to it to show her their way of life. We also visit Tenu and Njela, the two old ladies, one of them blind and the other one lame, at Mdori. They are overjoyed at seeing us again. We weep with them.

Our church at Mbuyu Jermani is more than full when we meet for a service on Sunday. All of the old Christians, except for a very few, are present. It does us good to see them once more. Marion and Doreen speak before I give the message. Many line up for prayer afterwards. The new songbook *Nyimbo za Ibada* (Hymns of Worship), which I had been working on while still in Tanzania, has finally been printed, and I brought 1,600 copies with me to leave with the church. I offer up the dedication prayer for the new songbook before handing them over to the executive. This is done again the following day at a service in Mirambo when we take Doreen to see Uburunge. Here James gives us a warm welcome.

We are treated like kings wherever we visit. Doreen receives many gifts from the Christians. Then it is time to return to Kenya. But, before we leave our old stamping grounds, Doreen is shown a Masai *boma*. This done, we travel on to Ngorongoro Crater, where we stop for our cup of tea. The view of the vast crater below with all its game is awe-inspiring each time I see it. We cannot stay long but must keep going if we are to reach Ibeno by tomorrow evening. Thus it is that we keep rolling until we arrive at Lobo Lodge, not stopping at Seronera as previously planned. We spot plenty of game, including lions, while travelling in the Serengeti National Park. The following day we cross the border into Kenya and stop at Keekorok Lodge for lunch. All kinds of game here, as always in the Masai-Mara Game Reserve. We finally reach our destination before dark. But before we can settle down from our long safari, Augustine and others show up and want to visit with us. While in Kenya, Doreen attends a service here at Ibeno, where I dedicate the new songbook *Nyimbo za Ibada*. I preach the message in English so that Doreen can understand it. My first time in Africa since launching out in Swahili, except once at the Kima Convention a few years ago.

We also take Doreen to Olereko in Masailand for a service. After feeding us, they put on a performance for us where they sing and the men hop up and down in their traditional fashion. Of course, they all look very colorful, especially the women in their beaded outfits. On our return trip we stop at Nyabitunwa, the border church, for our second service and more food. It is dark when we reach Ibeno. Before Doreen is done in Gusii, we take her to the stone grinding mill located only a few miles from Ibeno. It is run by a flowing stream.

What is a trip to Africa without a hunting safari! Doreen is game, and we plan one for Maji Moto, which is twenty-five miles beyond Narok, in Block 58A. The children are waiting when we pull in at RVA to pick them up. They are eager to get going on our weekend outing in the wilds.

The campsite is chosen beside a stream that is flowing from a hot-water spring only one-half of a mile away. Got up our tents by dark. Saw a lot of plains game while driving in, as well as Masai men traipsing about.

After breakfast, we commence our hunt. All of us go except for Marion, who stays behind to watch the camp. Too many Masai around. Colleen is after an eland. But we do not sight one, so she settles for a wildebeest, which she brings down with a single shot. We skin it out and haul the meat back to camp. A tall Masai accompanies us in the afternoon. He claims to know where there is a herd of eland not far from camp. And it is so. There is a big bull in the group that we immediately single out. We then commence our stalk. They do not allow us to get close, so I stop the vehicle to allow Colleen to make her shot. She drops the running bull with a well-placed shot. Colleen is ecstatic! She jumps up and down hugging me over and over. It is a nice trophy!

When the animal is skinned we head with the meat back to camp, where we hang it from a limb in the shade. The breeze will help form a coating over the meat that will keep it from spoiling for days. Any flies around will not be able to deposit their eggs in it as well. Before the day is done, Doreen manages to bag her first trophy in Africa. It is a Thomson gazelle. She is quite happy over it. A great day for the women, I must say!

We hear jackals and hyenas during the night. Doreen also discovers she has ants in her bedding. In the morning, Mark and I walk along the stream for dik-diks. Before long, we come across them and he shoots one. Then we head out for a wildebeest that Kirk needs. We do not have to travel far before a herd is spotted. A good-sized bull falls to Kirk's first shot! He is not about ready to have Colleen outdo him on the shooting range. The animal is skinned and the meat hauled back to camp. Excess meat has been given to the Masai who have been around camp since our arrival.

While we are eating our supper, the rain that has been threatening all afternoon comes down in torrents. It being dark outside, we do not notice the nearby stream filling up rapidly. Before we realize it, water is running into our tent! I discover it when I look down, from where I am seated at the table eating, the canvas floor ballooning upwards at my feet. As soon as we start walking, the water seeps in, and before we can get the bedding outside it is soaking wet.

When the rain begins to subside, we load all our stuff onto the roof rack of the Landcruiser. There is still much thunder and lightning. We pray that we will not get struck by one of the bolts. It is dangerous as we untie the meat from the limb of the tree where it has been hanging. We come through unscathed and it is 9:00 P.M. when we pull away from Maji Moto, drenched to our skin. The two-hour drive back to Kijabe in a pitch-black night over a trail that is mostly covered with pools of water wipes me out. As tired as we are, we first must clean up before sliding between the sheets here in the guest house.

We wake up refreshed and then work on the meat all forenoon. It is cut up, bagged and then stuck into the deep freeze, where it will stay until we leave for Ibeno. We give quite a bit of it to Kirk's dorm parent, as Kirk wants his fellow students to sample his prey. Marion washes our clothes and the bedding that got wet during yesterday's rain. Colleen does the ironing as soon as they are dry. At noon we have eland steak. It is delicious! The best meat around. Before Marion and I leave, we take the children up to their dorms. It is hard to leave them, especially Mark, as he begins to cry. Too soon our adventurous weekend together has come to an end. It is one that Doreen will not soon forget either.

Another hunting safari takes place north of Lake Baringo in Block 42. But before we can get there, we must check in at Kabarnet, where the game department has a post. The place is situated high up in the hills. We do not reach it until 6:00 P.M. Then it starts to rain heavily and our tenting equipment on the roof rack gets all wet. The game scout helps us find a place to spend the night. It is in the training center, which contains many bunks. They are all like hammocks, and so we end up with very little shut-eye.

The following day finds us on the shores of Lake Baringo. We pitch our tent at Kampi Ya Samaki near the bird sanctuary. The afternoon sun has the tent dried out in short order. We do not venture out on a hunt but spend it watching the hippo on the lake. Also, we talk to Leakey about animals to be found around here. He is presently involved in some project nearby. (His parents are the ones who discovered a primate skull at Olduvai Gorge back in 1959. They date it to be 2 million years old! Rather difficult to accept when one believes in the Biblical account of creation.)

Marion stays behind in camp when the children and I take off for the bush after breakfast. Hives are bothering her again, so she is only too happy to remain and watch our things. We drive north and turn east when clear of the lake. When we reach an *mbuga* (a treeless plain), we follow it north. Along the way we pick up a couple of natives who inform us that there are fringe-eared beisa about. We spot plenty of zebra and Grant gazelles and one lone eland, but no beisa. Then we come across some warthogs. Mark takes a shot and gets one with one bullet! He is improving with his aim and is not about to be left behind by his brother and sister.

We drive on farther, and then the water hose bursts! All the water from the radiator drains out. What to do? Right now we are in the middle of nowhere, miles away from camp. The two men whom we picked up tell us that there is a borehole about two miles away where the cattle herders bring their livestock to the water trough. We now need a container with which to fetch the water. This we have after dumping out our juice, which Marion prepared for our lunch. It is only a gallon in size, but it will help. Together with the gallon of water we have in another container, it should be enough to get us to the watering trough, where we can fill the radiator properly.

It is twelve noon when I send the men off for the water. Will they actually return? They may just take the container for themselves. We must believe they will come back with water. I have some tape, but it is not enough to close up the break in the hose. Then Kirk suggests we remove the tube from the spare tire, cut it into strips, and wrap it tightly around the broken hose. Great idea, Kirk! So we do that and two hours later, when the men return with the water, the hose is repaired.

After a word of prayer, we commence our journey back to camp. We dare not pick up a thorn for we now do not have a spare. On the way we drop off our Good Samaritans. Then we meet some local tribesmen who do not resemble any I have seen before. They may belong to the Dorobo tribe, who live off hunting and what they can gather in the bushes and forests. I try to converse with them, but I am not too successful. We carry on and reach camp without any further trouble. Praise the Lord!

We decide to pack up and pull out in the morning, as we cannot hunt with a patched-up water hose. This we do. When we reach Nakuru, I purchase a new water hose and a tube for the spare tire. Before carrying on with our hunt in another area near Kajiado, we stop at Kijabe for the night. The bed that we sleep in at the guest house that night is about the worst I have been in. Not only is it like a hammock, but the springs make a noise even when you breathe!

It is a nice day in Block 22C. We enjoy ourselves even though we do not get all we wanted. Colleen shoots a nice Grant gazelle with a good set of horns. Yes, she uses only a single bullet to kill the buck! Meanwhile, Kirk brings down a Thomson gazelle. Mark is after a wildebeest, but we do not come across any of them. But he will have a chance at one two weeks later when he gets his wildebeest in Block 21D near Athi.

Although a hunting safari provides us the greatest adventures, we do also make trips into the various game parks to take shots not with a gun, but with a camera. We visit Samburu Game Reserve and Meru National Park during one long weekend. To get there we must skirt Mount Kenya, the second-highest mountain in Africa. We see many different species of game in both of these places and take a swim in the pool at Buffalo Springs. The water contains some minerals. It was blasted out during the Second World War.

Olambwe Valley Game Reserve is only fifty miles west of Ibeno and quite near Lake Victoria. We see species of animals here that we have not seen previously in other parks. I wake up at midnight and find water dripping through the roof of the tent. When it keeps on raining, we move out. The boys finish their night in the vehicle, while Marion, Colleen, and I crawl into an empty building. Here it is dry, but mosquitoes disturb us the remaining part of the night.

The park that is about the best we have visited here in Kenya for its numerous species of animals is the Masai-Mara Game Reserve. It is second only to the Tarangire in Tanzania. On one visit we come upon many, many dead wildebeest piled up on rocks along the Mara River. It appears there was a flash flood here a week ago and as the wildebeest tried to cross many were swept to their death. When they are on migration nothing can stop them or deter them. The stench is almost unbearable! Vultures and marabou storks are so gorged on the rotting flesh that they are unable to get airborne. Crocodiles laze on the banks.

While I prefer to spend our vacations in a park viewing wildlife, Marion prefers the coast lying on a sandy beach. The children love both. And so it is that we find ourselves at Mombasa once in a while. Of course, the tent goes along with us even here. I remember the one trip when we arrive at 11:00 P.M. It takes us an hour to set the tent up in the dark, as it keeps on collapsing. We finally end up laughing and laughing at our failures of trying to fit the ends together in the light of a torch with batteries that were beginning to breathe their last.

In the morning we do not stay long but carry on to Malindi where we erect our tent on Silver Sands beach. Here we spend a lot of time in the water when the tide is in. A beautiful place! Then, it is off to Lamu farther up the coast. It is an Arab town situated on an island. We leave the Landcruiser on the mainland and cross over on a launch. It is different here; the streets are very narrow, only room enough for pedestrians, cyclists, and donkeys. There are no motor vehicles. Men are wearing the full-length white robes called *khanzus* and the *kofia* (caps), typically Islamic. The women cover themselves with the black wraparound called *bui bui*. Swahili is spoken throughout Lamu.

We find it very humid and crave water constantly. Our noonday meal consists of rice and goat meat eaten in a small restaurant. Lamu had a slave-based economy until that came to an end in 1907 with the abolition of slavery. It then slid into decline and has stayed that way ever since; thus their traditional style of architecture has remained undisturbed. This is also the island of legendary Sinbad the Sailor. On our return trip to Mombasa, we drop in and inspect the Gedi ruins. This ruined city dates back to the thirteenth century and has since been engulfed by a tropical forest. It had been settled by Arabs.

During our stay in Tanzania, we never made it to Zanzibar. So while in Mombasa, we book a flight and fly over to visit Spice Island. Zanzibar was once the largest slave port on the east coast of Africa. Nearly 50,000 slaves, from as far away as Lake Tanganyika, passed through its market each year. The Omani sultans ruled here until 1964, when they were overthrown, just prior to the union with mainland Tanganyika.

The streets are narrow and angle off every which way. Many buildings with brass-studded doors are standing empty. Previous owners have left the country since the government has nationalized businesses. Parts of the old stone city resemble a ghost town! The Sultan's Palace has become the People's Palace. We find many of the quaint little shops and bazaars deserted. Livingstone House still stands. It was Dr. Livingstone's base for his last expedition before he died.

We take a drive into the countryside to see the cinnamon, clove, and coconut plantations that cover much of the island. At the Old Slave Caves we stop and walk down into them. The place was used for illegal slave trading at one time, after the trade had been abolished by the British in the late 1800s. Then, when we hit an isolated spot along the coast, the children beg to take a swim in the water. They dash in without checking what is below the surface and step on top of sea urchins. Ouch! They scream and then scream some more as they make their painful way back to shore. Removing the spines proves to be not an easy job and several break off, their ends remaining embedded in the bottoms of the children's feet. They eventually will work their way out.

The hotel that we stay in on the island is an older one, and we eventually discover it does not have extra keys to some rooms. Colleen accidentally locks hers inside and now cannot enter her room. There is no ladder long enough to reach her window, which is on the third floor. So I come up with a plan, but it is quite dangerous. The boys' room is next to Colleen's. I have Mark climb outside his window and then inch his way along a narrow ledge till he reaches her window. Even with me hanging onto him, it is very scary. I do not breathe until Mark is safely inside her room.

Once we are back in Mombasa, we visit Gerald and Ellen Stevenson, missionaries who are living here on the coast. Their son, Timothy, and Colleen have been dating each other recently, as much as RVA will allow them, which is not much according to the couple. On the way back to Nairobi we pass through Tsavo National Park. There is a stretch in here where once man-eating lions terrorized the crew during the building of the railroad at the end of the last century.

Then, we are back at Ibeno again, back with the crowds. But we have been revived to tackle the work with renewed energy. To be away from people crowding in around you has been refreshing and needful.

Chapter Eighteen
Hunting Safaris

We hunt for two reasons. The first is that we prefer wild meat, as it is healthier than that from the local domesticated animals. It contains no pesticides and next to no cholesterol, which cannot be said for beef and pork. The second reason is it provides an outing where we can get away from it all, retreat to the bush, and just enjoy the outdoors, listening to the dove cooing in the treetop or to the howl of the hyena at dusk. How precious these moments have been to me throughout the years in Tanzania. And I now look forward to them here in Kenya.

Colleen began her hunting back in Tanzania. Her first animal was as impala that she dropped with her first shot. Then came reedbuck, waterbuck, hartebeest, wildebeest, warthogs, and Grant and Thomson gazelles, just to mention some. Kirk soon followed and he proved to be a good shot as well. As for Mark, he was only nine when we left Tanzania, so he had not really started yet, except for small stuff and birds, which the other two had shot also.

My first hunt in Kenya, as it turns out to be, is with Merv Thomas. What a coincidence! My first hunt in Tanzania (Tanganyika then) fifteen years ago was with Merv. It is good to be on a hunt with him again. We go out to Block 59, which is just off the main road going towards Narok. There is plenty of game, and I end up shooting a *kongoni* (hartebeest) for myself and another one for Merv. Sheila, his wife, is with us, and she has brought along lunch, which we take time to eat before returning to Nairobi, where they are now stationed.

Our first trip to the bush as a family is to Block 60, which is not far from Ibeno, just beyond our churches in Masailand. We take along our tent and set up camp near the Migori River. The children are with me as I set out to bag my first topi, an animal I did not shoot in Tanzania, as I never came across them on any of my hunting safaris. We see a good selection of animals and then topi. I crawl up to the herd in the tall grass and from behind a termite mound I drop one of the bulls with a single shot. Everyone is pleased that it happened so quickly.

We have come for two days, and during this time we run across plenty of game, including buffalo and elephants on several different occasions. We hear the tuskers on both nights. Their screams can either thrill you or frighten a year's growth out of you! The meat from the two legs of the topi have been cut into strips and hung on a line to dry in the sun. The children are making jerky to take with them back to school. Masai *morani* have been stopping by, always curious and checking on what we are up to in the bush. Before we head home, I shoot an oribi, which are numerous in this area, but tricky to get.

On our next safari to Block 60, Colleen brings down a *kongoni* with her first shot. We see a lot of game, but the boys are unable to get a good bead on what I have on the license. Near the escarpment, I manage to shoot a nice warthog, which I thought was big until we spot another one a few days later near Lolgorien. When the boys and Colleen point him out to me, I take him for a rhino. But after he brings up his head there is no mistake. It is a warthog and a big one at that. His tusks are huge! I can hardly believe my eyes. I hear the children whispering, "Shoot; shoot." So I do, finally. The warthog does not know what hits him and drops with one bullet. He carries the largest tusks I have ever gotten, and also seen for many years.

Kirk and Mark are successful on the following safari in Block 60. An impala finally falls after three shots by Mark, and Kirk has to walk some before he gets his oribi. Colleen is after an eland, but it is difficult to find a decent male in the herds we come across. Just the same, we keep trying and walk at least five miles after one herd without firing a shot. We return to camp after dark and in the rain. It is our nineteenth wedding anniversary, and Marion pretty well was alone all day! No cake with special trimmings out here in the bush. We return home with one more animal, a Defassa waterbuck, which I dropped across the river from camp. It carried a good set of horns.

During our hunting safaris in Block 60, we have come across buffalo each time. When I finally get my .458 rifle from the police, after a long-drawn out hassle with the game department where I had to prove in writing from their counterpart in Tanzania that I had hunted big game, I take out a license for three buffalo. The German vet in Kisii accompanies me on my first outing for buffalo in Kenya. We come across them on the banks of the Migori River, just across from where the family and I camped in August.

We stalk them on foot and when close enough to shoot they are off on the run. My bullet enters a bull's chest cavity and slows him down. He manages to stagger into a thicket before I have another opportunity to pull the trigger. We know he is waiting for us inside, but there is no alternative. I must go in and finish him off. That is the rule! The vet fans out to my right while I move towards the thicket straight on. I enter and discover the wounded buffalo is right ahead of me almost hidden in the thick foliage. He is in the process of getting up, for he had been lying down, and then he charges! The vet and I both shoot and this time the bull stays down.

Since I have room on my license for more, we carry on.

It is not long before we spot them in an opening across a ravine. We move cautiously down into the depression, which is densely overgrown with tall grass and bush, plenty of cover for a herd and especially for a mean bull ready to pick a fight. It seems forever before we break cover. Too late, they catch our scent and disappear into the woods. We have come out on the wrong side of them. In the process of retracing our steps to the vehicle we miss it among the stand of trees, which look so much alike. When we finally find it, it is time for us to return home with the meat.

Kupper, the German vet, is with me again as I return to the bush for the remaining two buffalo. I drive all the way to the escarpment, turn left onto a trail, and travel until we come to a hill. Here we leave the vehicle and commence walking into the stand of trees. We have walked only a short distance when I spy a buffalo in some covering. He is a big bull with a good set of horns. My .458 slug slams into his chest, and he comes to life. He dashes into the next thicket to conceal himself, but it isn't enough. I place another bullet into him, and he drops in his tracks. Kupper then puts one in to make sure. The horns measure over forty-four inches!

There must be more around. And there is. A bull rushes out of a thicket right in front of me. He is broadside to me and only fifteen yards away. I plant a slug into his chest as he is about to pass by. The buffalo turns and charges towards me. There is a tree behind me, and when I give him my second bullet the recoil drives me against it. Ahead of me I see the bull take the full impact of the bullet and he goes to his knees. Then, ever so slowly, the rest of him sinks to the ground. The buffalo is dead. Only six yards separate us! I would not want it any closer.

What do we do with all the meat? There is a seminar on at the time, and we pass much of it on to them. It never goes lost. If there is not a convention or seminar in progress, then the workers at the compound will snatch up what we cannot handle. In Tanzania, our Bible school benefitted much from my hunts.

Fred and Emma Mehrer with their two children, Melody and Dwayne, visit us for a week, and during their stay we take them to our favorite hunting grounds—Block 60. Fred and Emma were the youth counselors when I attended the church near Churchbridge, Saskatchewan, years ago. It is nice to visit with them again. We are camping at our usual spot near the Migori River. Colleen right off gets her topi with one shot. It is a big one. I miss out on a klipspringer again. They have eluded me all this time. But I do bring down a nice big male bushbuck near camp.

Kirk has no trouble with a zebra and drops him with one bullet. Mark and Colleen each get an oribi. Dwayne Mehrer does well on his try at wild game in Africa and shoots a hartebeest. He makes only one shot with the 30-06. We see buffalo in the evening near camp, but Colleen and I are unable to approach them close enough for a shot. She wishes to shoot one this time around. We will try again tomorrow while the two boys stay behind with their mom and prepare some jerky to take to school.

Early in the morning I take Colleen to where we saw the buffalo last night. But there is no trace of them. After breakfast we head out for the escarpment. The Mehrer family are with us. We see elephants along the way. Licenses for them are not available here in Kenya. As we approach the escarpment, we spot a lone bull just off the road about 150 yards away. It appears he has just emerged from the bush. There may be more inside. There is no cover between us and the buffalo. Colleen will have to take a shot from here. It is unbelievable yet true! The bull drops with her first shot from the 30-06.

We carry on closer, but there is no further movement. I get her to give him another slug. But it was not necessary. The

186

animal is stone dead. She is all excited and happy at the same time! The bullet entered the eye and passed into the brain. The bull must have held his head at the right angle for her to have pulled off this shot. I had my .458 backing her all along, but she did not need my help to get her first buffalo. She did it all by herself. What a shot! And what a gal.

Her joy almost turns into tragedy when, only a few hours later, while helping me in the search for a klipspringer on the escarpment, she narrowly misses sliding down a jagged cliff to her death. We had split up a few minutes ago and I had just passed around a corner in the rocks when I hear a scream followed by my name being called. I scramble to find her, and at first I cannot see her. Then I hear her call me in a weak voice and it is coming from below me. I peer over the side of the cliff, and find her hanging onto a sapling, her feet dangling in space!

My heart is in my throat as I ever so carefully reach out my hand to grab her wrist before the sapling pulls out by the root. Should I dislodge any rocks they will smash into her upturned face. I grasp her hand and gently pull her up onto solid ground. We step back from the edge and hang onto one another until the shock wears off. I notice then that she has a big gash on her shin bone. It is bleeding and there is a lot of dirt inside the cut. I try to draw out as much as I can with my mouth. Then I tie my handkerchief over the gash to stop the bleeding. I half carry her back to the vehicle where the Mehrers are waiting.

Colleen now relates what had happened. While she was waiting for me to return, the flat rock she was standing on slid from under her. She went over the side with it and would have tumbled hundreds of feet before hitting bottom. But in reaching out she clutched a sapling, which stopped her descent. Thank the Lord it held until I was able to grab her wrist. Her leg was gashed on the rocks when she slid over the edge of the cliff.

At camp Marion takes a look at the ugly cut on Colleen's foot and decides it should be properly cleaned out and then stitched. This means taking her to the hospital at Kilgoris. So off we go to have it done. There is no painkiller and Colleen puts up quite a fuss when the medical officer scrubs out the gash, snips off the torn vessels, and then puts in five stitches. Ouch! It hurts me just watching it. We return to camp before dark.

During the night a leopard has a feed on some of our meat hanging from the trees near our tent. His tracks are visible in the morning.

Of course, Kirk now wants a buffalo as well. He cannot let big sister get the best of him. He is not quite fifteen yet, much too young to tackle a buffalo. But I relent and we drive out to Lolgorien for his buffalo. Mark comes along. By one o'clock we find two of them out in the open. Kirk takes a bead on the head of the biggest one with the 30-06 and fires. But the bull does not go down this time when the bullet hits him on the side of the head. Instead he lumbers off into a thicket where I plant a .458 slug into his ribs. He charges out straight for the vehicle. I manage to slip out of his way in time.

The wounded animal makes for another thicket. It does not have sufficient undergrowth for him to hide in. As the bull is exposed, Kirk pumps in several more bullets. The bull finally goes down. We wait a few minutes, and then we hear him give the bellow of death. I walk in with the big gun to check. Behind me I hear Kirk saying, "Be careful, Dad; he may still be alive!" But I find him dead. To make sure I put a .458 bullet into him. I remember someone somewhere saying, "It is the dead ones that kill you." So now Kirk has his buffalo!

We make plans to go on a crocodile hunt up in northeastern Kenya in Block 7. Crocodiles are still plentiful in many parts of East Africa. They were there in Tanzania, but I never was able to get a license for one. So here was my chance to bag me one. Our destination is Merti, on the Ewaso Nyiro River. Here the river narrows and crocodiles are numerous. In fact, livestock are taken by them and, at times, humans as well when they come for water. The Boran tribe lives out here with their camels, cattle, and goats.

To get there we travel past Mount Kenya, continuing north until we reach Archer's Post. Then we turn off right and jog over a dirt road in a northeasterly direction. The first night, we camp beside the river under some palm trees. Monkeys are everywhere, setting up a constant chatter. The Ewaso Nyiro is wide here, sandy and shallow. This place is called Kleinmaster's Camp. In the evening many Boran children bring in their livestock, including camels, which carry tinkling bells around their long necks, to drink at the water's edge. After dark a herd of buffalo come to quench their thirst and then hang around for a long time. We hear hyenas and lions.

The boys and I check for buffalo in the morning. Finding no trace of them, we return and take down our tent. Then we are off to Merti. Many Boran villages along the way. Their huts resemble haystacks—like those of the Tindiga tribe in Tanzania. Very hot and dry here. At Merti we are told to continue farther up the river until we reach a large pool. There we find our crocodiles and hippos as well. I shoot one of them. It disappears under the water. When I again see a croc, I place a bullet between its eyes. Was it the one I shot previously? I cannot tell. Then a big croc surfaces and we know this one is a different one. It is Colleen's turn and she makes a good shot. The crocodile surfaces after a short stay underwater. We pull it out of the water and measure it. Twelve feet! That is a good one. Then Kirk has a go at one and he also makes an excellent shot. It comes up almost immediately. When it is pulled onto the bank the length is nine feet. We fail to get them skinned before dark.

We hear hippos grunting all night long. The crocodiles that Colleen and Kirk shot are still lying where we left them last night. We also find two crocs floating in the river, the ones I shot yesterday. So they were two different ones! They are ten- and eleven-footers. It takes until noon to skin them out. Another hot day! Millions of doves and sandgrouse flock in at dusk to drink at the water's edge. It is something to behold; as many as there are, they never collide while descending and ascending. We eat crocodile meat for supper. It is white in color and tastes like fish.

Elephants come to drink before we retire for the night. Later on they did a lot of screaming and trumpeting. We also hear the lions and hyenas, but they are distant. In the morning I walk down to the river to check for tracks. Mark is with me. On the way back to camp, I spy three Grevy's zebras walking along the riverbed where it is day. By crouching I am able to come abreast of them without their suspecting anything. I hit the big stallion with my first shot. He runs only a few steps when my second bullet drops him. I have my Grevy's zebra before breakfast! He is a beauty.

We load our stuff and leave Merti at noon. We pick up some drinking water at the village, as we have been boiling the water from the pool and drinking it even though it is brown, dirty, and slimy! At Kittermaster's Camp we pick a nice spot right beside the river and set up our tent on the bank. That done, we take a wash in the shallow river. The water is actually warm. It has been another hot, hot day! A lot of baboons around. We hear lions as we bed down for the night. Then there is a lot of noise when the buffalo cross the river.

During the night a leopard takes some of our meat we had forgotten outside. His tracks are there for us to see. We see waterbuck and gerenuk on our walks along the river and into the bush. When we meet up with dik-diks, Mark downs one with the .22 rifle. I still need to get a fringe-eared beisa before we vacate this hunting block. We leave Kittermaster's Camp and follow the river as it turns deeper into the bush. When we set up camp for the night we are at least two miles from the dirt road. I take a dip in the river and later discover a hippo is occupying the same water I just came from!

We hear the splash of the water after dark as the hippo walks along in the shallow river. In the morning we discover his tracks as he passed our tent only twenty feet away! We spend the day searching for the fringe-eared beisa, but by evening we still have not come across any. The hippo is still around, but we take a dip in the water anyway, of course, keeping a wary eye on him. He may be getting used to us by now.

After dark the lions start grunting nearby. By eight they are near the tent. Our tent is pitched at the edge of the bank on a path that is running parallel to the river. One of the lions coming up this path suddenly discovers our tent blocking his way. He surveys the situation for a while and then bounds past the corner, tripping on the guiderope. It shakes the whole tent! All of us inside bolt upright from where we were lying on our sleeping bags. All eyes are as huge as saucers. We put out the light and wait, my .458 ready in my hand. It is very still outside. We dare not move, expecting at any moment the lion to come crashing into our tent!

When there is no further movement, I shine my torch through the side opening. There in the light I see a lioness sitting not ten yards away staring back at me! Where is the male? I move the torch around, but I fail to locate him in the darkness. I switch off the light. More tense waiting. He is out there somewhere alright; that is why she is still around. There might be a full pride discussing the prospects of a full-course meal. I am ready, the torch in one hand and the .458 in the other. I do not have a license for a lion, but I will not hesitate to shoot should they charge the tent.

Marion and Mark drop off to sleep, but Colleen and Kirk are too tense to follow their example. The 30-06 is in easy reach for either one to use should it be necessary. There is some rustling outside until about eleven and then nothing more from the lions. Colleen and Kirk started to doze after midnight. I can hear the hippo wandering around in the riverbed until about five in the morning. I have had an uneasy night, catching only a few winks between three and five. I remember looking at my watch at twenty minutes after four. It is good to see the light of day again. Time to unwind.

The tracks of the male lion are plain to see where he walked up the path till he was near the tent. Then his dash past us. He must not have noticed the rope, for he ran right into it. We will not easily forget this night! After breakfast we load up and pull out of this remote area. Had something happened to us no one would have found us for weeks, for as I mentioned earlier, we had driven in at least two miles, without following any track, from the dirt road that we were on.

Once we are back on the main road we head for home. We have had an exciting hunting safari! And with a lot of extra thrown in for good measure, I must add.

Chapter Nineteen
Farewell, Africa!

Not only do we plant new churches in Masailand, but new ones are started in Gusii as well. It is a thrill to see new converts won for Christ in the remote areas of this populous tribe. As we near the end of our ministry in Kenya, an old woman who is a diviner repents and accepts Christ. After the service she shuffles over to a nearby hut and fetches us her gourd containing stones that she has been using in her profession. Truly, a sign she is abandoning her practice of divining! A similar conversion took place in Tanzania just before our departure when an old witch doctor surrendered his life to Christ. These are wonderful farewell gifts the Lord has given us before we leave each country!

Because the work is much older in Kenya than in Tanzania, we have found pastors who are up in years. They are not rushed in the way they conduct their services. Announcements can take up a lot of time. More minutes are wasted when the offering is counted so precisely. At times, the services will have their humorous moments as well. Since most of them love wearing eye glasses, they are often not their size. We have seen them fall off more than once when the pastors or song leaders lead the service.

We discover the youth love to sing. It isn't long before we are holding choir contests between the churches in their districts. During these occasions we hear some beautiful singing. The finalists from the districts compete in the annual youth convention at Ibeno. Here the overall winner is declared. The young people of Gusii are very competitive and show up in droves.

A service I will long remember is the one at Getacho where I preached on dedicating our children. When I finally got done praying for the last child, there were seventy-six of them! I have never had that many dedicated to the Lord in a single service prior to this occasion. Here in Gusii, as in Masailand, children are given our names, especially the ones where Marion has assisted their mothers in bringing them into the world.

The new building for the secondary school at Ibeno gets under way during our final year in Kenya. We do not see its completion, but we are present on Harambee Day, when the member of parliament and the permanent secretary challenge the crowd of 1,000-plus to come up with enough money and materials to finish the structure. The goal is reached. To show their appreciation for a job well done as treasurer, the committee gives me a farewell party with the chief in attendance. I am given a big Kisii stool, and Marion receives a beaded bag. The set of *World Books* that my sister Doreen sent recently I now donate to the secondary school.

Most of the women in the preschool clinic give Marion a wonderful farewell. They form a circle around her and do a tribal dance with lots of singing. She is honoured with speeches and gifts. It is a highlight in Marion's ministry during our term in Kenya assisting mothers with a healthier diet for their malnourished children. She will miss the clinics.

Soon after our arrival here in southwestern Kenya, we are invited to Chemosit, situated in the land of the Kipsigis, bordering the Gusii to the northeast. Here we find the beginnings of a church. Marion and I visit several homes where we listen to their needs and pray for them. At one place we discover a man who has a water-driven grinding mill made out of stone, much like the one at Ibeno. We spend the night in a nearby guest house.

The following day, which is Sunday, there is a service in the church with about one hundred in attendance. Marion and I sing a duet before I preach the message, which is translated into Kipsigis by one of the men. After I have prayer for the nineteen who come forward, Marion has a short meeting with the women. Before we leave, we are invited to return again. Not just once, but on a regular basis. We would love to oblige, but the Lord directs our footsteps into Masailand instead.

Chiggers are quite common in tropical Africa. They resemble fleas and breed in the dust and dirt of dwellings where livestock and poultry are housed. When females come in touch with a bare foot, they burrow under the skin, where they then feed on the soft tissues. In the end they swell up to the size of a small pea as eggs grow inside. This is the time to remove them, before the skin ulcerates and breaks open, leaving a sore which then may become seriously infected.

Where chiggers are common, people become very skilful in removing them. This we have discovered each time we are infected with one, especially Marion, who loves wearing open-toed shoes and sandals. She will call one of the women on the station, who then digs out the chiggers in no time at all. Mothers are experts at it, maybe because of all the practice they receive removing them from their own children. The few times I pick up the pesky fleas, I prefer digging them out myself.

I love honey and finally, here at Ibeno, I hang up my own hive. African bees are active even in the cool season. So it is that soon we have plenty of it on the table. Not the brown stuff that is mixed with dead bees and debris brought to us by honey hunters from the forest, but beautiful clear honey. But there is a price to pay. In spite of wearing a net over my head, I usually get stung several times before I am through lifting out the honey from the hive.

One night bees manage to enter through a tear in my gear and I am stung on the side of my head at least twenty times before I free myself from them. Then, while working on the honey, I am stung again by those that follow me inside the house. When I begin to feel the effects of the poison in my system, Marion feeds me a lot of vitamin C to help ease the allergic reaction. This vitamin is an antioxidant that reduces the effects of allergy-producing substances. It is touch and go for a while, but I pull through the critical stage and am fine by morning. The next time I am stung as often again, I immediately take vitamin C and do not get sick.

It always amazes me how many stings the honey hunters can take. I have seen my tracker covered with bees while out after elephant in Tanzania as he extracted the honey from a hole in the tree. He did not mind them, just let them swarm around his head. Because he did not beat the air, they did not get angry with him. After it was all over, he smeared honey over the places the bees had stung him. That is all! The old watchman here on the station assists me with the honey extraction. He wears a long coat, but his feet are bare and this is where the bees sting him. This makes him hop around a bit. But he is careful to keep his hands in his pockets.

Marion takes time to do a lot of baking for the children when we go out to see them for the long weekend. When it is birthday time there is a special cake for them. She makes sure it is different each time. While preparing for one of their homecomings, she tries in vain to find some ground millet for Mark, as he prefers porridge made from this grain above all the rest. She had sent the workers to the nearby markets but they returned empty.

It is a disappointment to Marion, maybe more so with her

than it would have been to Mark. But God cares, even in the little things of life. Several women from a village some distance away drop in for a short visit. They have brought Marion a gift. It is ground millet! The women did not know that she had been looking for some and were as happy as Marion when she explained the reason why. God granted her the wish.

While I was hustling around one evening getting stuff ready for our trip the next day to take the children back to school, my small toe catches the end of the settee and almost gets ripped off! After I quit hopping around, I check to see if it is broken. It certainly looks like it, as I can bend it over sideways and backwards. What are Marion and Colleen up to while I am in excruciating pain? Enjoying a good laugh! I suppose I did look funny hopping on one leg while holding onto the other.

My toe and foot are quite sore in the morning. I wore a sock for the night so as to avoid snagging the broken toe each time I moved. It is difficult to walk on it, but I do and we head out for Kijabe. The trip is a painful one, and when we arrive I stop at the hospital only to find the doctor out. I need an X ray to find out what is what with the toe. We carry on to Colleen's dormitory and unload her trunk from the roof rack. The children help me with it. Then it is off to Mark's dorm. Here I discover there is no more pain in my left foot. I squeeze my little toe and no pain! The Lord has answered prayer and healed it. Thank You! No more limping.

The children enjoy RVA. It is home away from home. The station is situated on an escarpment around seven thousand feet high and overlooks the Rift Valley. There is a breathtaking view, where one can almost look into the extinct volcano Mount Longonot, lying just below. Kirk and I finally take the time to climb it during a weekend when Colleen is away with the other Grade 12s at Mombasa on Senior Safari. Mark stays behind with Marion. We easily climb the 9,120-foot mountain and the view of the crater inside is beautiful. It is 590 feet deep, with a diameter of two and a half miles.

The railway line passes through Kijabe. I caught the train from Kisumu to Nairobi once and passed by the school in early morning. It was a good experience. A dense forest surrounds the station where RVA is located. After the Mau-Mau revolt in 1952, the place was often in danger of attack. While hunting in Block 60, I met someone from another hunter's camp who shared with me the following story when he heard that we have children attending RVA.

The man, a Kikuyu, belonged to the much-feared fighters who hid out in the Mau-Mau forest. They fought to drive out the white man from their farms in the highlands. So many atrocities were committed! One night he found himself with a group of Mau-Mau (as they now were known) on their way to RVA for the sole purpose of putting to an end all those on the station. The men slip out of the forest and make their way to the buildings. Then, an incredible thing takes place that sends fear through their hardened hearts and they quake at the sight before them.

Huge figures in white are surrounding the station. A halo of light illuminates them. The men turn with fright and disappear into the forest, one trying to outrun the other. No one wants to be the last one! The man telling me the story runs through the night, a feat only possible because of the horror of being caught by one of those glowing giants. He finally drops exhausted on the doorstep of someone's home. The owner, the pastor of a church near Naivasha, discovers him at daybreak.

It is only after he has poured out his story to the preacher and is prayed for that the man who has told me of his experience finds peace in his heart. God was looking after His flock at RVA and had set guardian angels to keep watch over them. The hardened Mau-Mau had failed in their mission of death. How often those guardians from above have held back the enemy from entering RVA, before and since that day, we may never know. Marion and I always have the assurance each time we leave our children behind at school He will look after them.

In one of Colleen's letters, she informs us of her spiritual experience she had when she rededicated herself in a service where a guest speaker brought the message. She sounds so happy! Marion and I rejoice with her. Colleen sings in the choir when it presents "Celebrated Life" at a concert we do not fail to attend. She makes the first team on the hockey squad. The following year she is chosen to be the captain. While Colleen excels in field hockey, Kirk does well in the soccer team that he plays with in his league.

At the sports banquet in her last year at school, she wins the MVP (Most Valuable Player) award in hockey! In volleyball she receives an award as well. I am really proud of her! She is getting to be better in sports than I ever was. Colleen also does very well in the Homecoming Queen competition, where she is chosen senior attendant. That's next to the queen! The boys are as proud of her as Marion and I are.

We plan to leave Africa immediately after Colleen's graduation day at RVA. This means our farewell service with the Gusii takes place at Ibeno just prior to her memorable event. All the pastors and church elders in Gusii are present for the service. The chief is here, plus the medical staff. The tabernacle on the station is packed out. There are decorations everywhere. Marion and I are escorted into the building as though we are a couple going to a wedding and then again out after the service, which is three and a half hours long!

A lot of fine words are said, including some from the chief. Soon after our arrival he had told me that the mission should be more involved with the needs around it. This we tried to do during our stay at Ibeno, which he now applauded me for. Marion and I receive very nice gifts. I am given a vest made out of skin by the youth. It is one they used to wear years ago at weddings. The pastors present me with a colobus monkey skin hat, which only very brave men wore. I feel very honoured!

The youth give Marion a plate and a bowl made from Kisii stones which is native to this locality. From the area she is presented with a marriage anklet ring and the name *Kwamboka* is conferred upon her, which in Kigusii means "crossing the water." They explain that she came from across the ocean and now is married to the tribe. Quite an honour! She receives a table cloth from the women with "Kwamboka" embroidered into the middle of it. More choir numbers follow before the service finally concludes.

There is another gift that we receive, which is a big eight-stringed lyre, called the *obokhano* in their language. This kind of musical instrument has been around for years. (One was found in a pyramid in Egypt.) Someone plays it for us and sings lyrics of our accomplishments during our stay in Gusii. It is all spontaneous. And so end our years in Kenya. We hope that what we have done will have been for the betterment of His kingdom in the country. We enjoyed doing it!

At RVA we pack all our suitcases before the graduation exercises commence so that we are ready to leave right after everything is over. I take time to compose a graduation letter to my daughter. There is a tinge of sadness in my heart in spite of this being a joyous occasion. It is hard to believe that our little girl has become a young lady! She has completed twelve years of schooling and is now ready to go off to college. Time has slipped by much too quickly and there is no way of turning back the clock.

The audience stands as the sixty-two graduates file into the chapel to the strains of "My Africa." Colleen looks lovely as she marches up the aisle. There are tears in her eyes as there are in mine and Marion's. The service is very nice! I have to weep several times. Eighteen years of cherished memories keep going through my mind. Then it is time for the graduates to receive their diplomas. Every proud parent now rushes forward to take pictures. When it is all over, we gather in the dining hall for a bite to eat.

At three o'clock we leave for Nairobi. Colleen drives along with the Stevensons, as today is her last day with Tim. He is taking it quite hard. They remain with us until we check in at the airport. Solomon Sumbe comes in all the way from Tanzania to see us off! The plane, an El Al airliner from Israel, leaves one and a half hours late. The delay is on purpose, as luggage is thoroughly checked. Security police surround the plane as we board it in total darkness. We can just make out their armored vehicles.

The heavy security is due to retaliatory threats made by Palestinians to blow up one of the Israeli airliners. It hasn't been long since Israel successfully masterminded an air raid on Entebbe airport in next-door Uganda and rescued the passengers of a plane that the Palestinians had hijacked. Therefore, the need for all these precautionary measures.

We lift off at 10:00 P.M. tired and worn out. Marion and I leave with thoughts of not returning, even though we have been invited to come back to Kenya by its church leaders. Our priorities are with our children right now, and we feel we need to be nearby when Colleen enters college life. Farewell, Africa!

Chapter Twenty

What Next?

Our short stay in the Holy Land is a memorable one. We had visited it back in 1965 when Mark was just a baby. This time the children are older and able to comprehend more, especially Colleen, of the meaning of all the historical sites we visit. Again, the Bible becomes very alive to Marion and me. As we stand in the Garden of Gethsemane, our thoughts return to the day our Lord prayed for strength to drink that bitter cup. My heart overflows with gratitude, as it did on our previous visit, when we bow and thank Him for successfully completing His mission to bring us salvation.

This time there is a two-hour security check at Tel Aviv Airport before departure. We, as a family, pass through quite easily due to being missionaries, but not so with many others.

The El Al airliner arrives two hours late in Istanbul, Turkey. Here we tour the city and are amazed at the many mosques that dot the skyline! Many of them used to be Orthodox churches. We cross the long bridge into Asian Turkey for a look. Then it is off to Athens, Greece, where we visit the Acropolis with all its ruins of ancient temples. Among others we also stop at Mars Hill, where the Apostle Paul shared Jesus with the philosophers of that time.

Eventually we land in Vancouver, where we are met by Marion's folks and others. So now we are back in Canada! What the future holds for us God only knows. As it unfolds itself, may we find favor in His sight. We certainly need His guidance, as we want His will to be done in our lives always. What kind of tracks, if any, will we be making here in the homeland when once our furlough is completed?

Three weeks later finds us in Anderson, Indiana. We check in at the missionary furlough apartment, which turns out to be an old house that eventually is moved away to make room for the new apartment block. Once we have Colleen settled in Anderson College (now University) and the boys in their respective schools, I commence touring the churches that have faithfully supported us through the years. Marion joins me whenever she can. During the months that follow, we do not have the slightest idea where we will live and what we will do when our furlough ends and our leave of absence begins. What next?

To begin with, while still in Kenya, I was thinking of going into a wildlife or conservation program in Canada. I had enrolled in a conservation course at the National School of Conservation out of New Jersey and graduated with a diploma. I could not imagine being stuck behind a pulpit in some church after having spent years in the great outdoors making tracks in the dust. No, a pastorate would be difficult for me to settle into.

So I searched elsewhere, sending for literature on land we could homestead in northern British Columbia. We sat for hours at Ibeno and planned our future home. I still have the plans for our house I dreamed of building, with the children each having his or her very own room, with plenty of space throughout the house to display all our curios and gifts that the people have given us. Then, there was the trophy room. But it does not materialize. The Lord is not in it. I know enough that if He does not approve of it then forget it. I keep searching for His will. What next?

While in the States, I keep my eyes open for a ranch

somewhere in the southwest. During a lull in our itineration, I fly to New Mexico for a look at a spread that is for sale near the Continental Divide. Maybe we can do some ranching? I know something about it, as I spent time with cattle and horses during my early years in Saskatchewan. The children are keen on this plan as well. But, again, the witness of the Lord is missing. Even when, as a family, we travel through the western states on itinerations, nothing turns us on. What next?

Nearing the end of our furlough, after the Lord has allowed me sufficient time to exhaust my will for our future, He begins directing me to continue on in the ministry. At what? I had investigated the possibility of working with the American Indians and enquired about it at Home Missions in Anderson but was told there was no opening. Where next? While we are in Colorado, one of the churches is looking for a pastor. After the service, we are told that they will keep in touch with us, as there are other candidates seeking the post. The children are happy with what they see, and so is Marion. There is even a house on an acreage that appeals to us, and it is for sale.

Our furlough expires the end of July 1977, just as we arrive back in Canada. Our eighteen years as missionaries have now come to an end. What next? In a month's time Colleen must be back in Anderson College and the boys must enter school somewhere. We pull in at Marion's folks' house to wait out the month. Maybe the church in Colorado will call and tell us that I have been accepted. But it is Carstairs, Alberta, that calls and asks me to be their pastor. I stall and answer Floyd Allenbrand that I must pray about it. He said that's fine but would we come and see the place?

We do drop in on our way to Edmonton, where we have planned a visit with my sister Doreen and her family. I had been to Carstairs earlier when itinerating, never dreaming then that I would be back considering the possibility of being their pastor. We leave without giving them an answer. I do tell Floyd that I will call in a week's time. To this, he says they need to know by Sunday morning at the latest.

Upon our return to Vernon, I call Colorado and am told that there is a tie in the votes. Could I return for another service? That does it! This must not be the Lord's will. If He wants me to be the pastor of that church in Colorado, then there should not be this horse race! I tell them to remove my name.

Now what about Carstairs? Does He want us there? If so, He needs to make it very real. Marion says it is out of the question! We discuss it and pray, and then discuss it some more. Then it is Saturday evening. Carstairs needs to know tonight! Tomorrow morning at the latest, we had been told. We go to bed, but I cannot sleep. I drop on my knees beside the bed and commence seeking the Lord's will. I soon lose track of time.

It is two in the morning when the Lord witnesses very definitely that we are to accept the call to Carstairs. I awaken Marion and brief her on what happened. She cannot believe her ears. "You will have to go by yourself then," she says. I ask her to pray as I did. And so it is that He lays the burden on her heart as well that Carstairs will be our next home. I call Floyd in the morning, and before we know it Gary Kellsey's truck arrives to move our belongings to Carstairs. Our boys are enrolled in school and Colleen is off to Anderson.

Carstairs is a small town nestled near the foothills and surrounded by ranches. My favorite singer of yesteryears, Wilf Carter, the yodeling cowboy, once lived just down the road from here. The members in the church are so gracious and helpful to the whole family. They receive us with open arms. Any reservations that Marion and I had about coming to pastor here soon evaporate. They are patient with me as I readjust to leading a local flock from overseeing a vast number of them. How different it is to see the same faces every week all week long!

My messages on missions must have been interesting to begin with, but I am guessing it was getting too much eventually to hear of Africa that often. But I manage to make the switch. Without His assistance, it would not have been possible. As I prepare new messages, I have experiences that take me to the gates of heaven! These are precious times that I have with the Lord up in my office, and then at the altar in the sanctuary. I meet Him there each Sunday morning for an anointing before anyone arrives. It becomes my Holy of Holies!

Even though Marion and I were born and raised in Canada, the eighteen-year absence from the ministry in the Canadian field is quite a gap to span immediately. Not only do I have to switch in the kind of messages I preach, but I find conversational interests differ vastly! Whereas local concerns are high on their priority list, my concerns are other lands and their culture. I am in the dark many times when my parishioners converse about local affairs. And so, slowly by slowly, Marion and I have to learn again how to be like the Romans if we are going to live with them. Canadians that is. Aye?

We soon discover that the telephone can take the place of prayer. It is much easier and handier to call the doctor or nurse than to get down and pray, much easier to take medication than to believe the Lord for healing. There is nothing wrong with doctors and medicines, but Marion and I coming from an area where there was little access to both, God had become the source of our health and healing. Not just for us only, but for the people we worked with in Africa as well. I find myself preaching on faith and believing God for miracles. Then one day, the Lord uses me in an experiment of what faith can do.

Ice hockey is the national sport in Canada. It is not only

my favorite game, but that of countless others. When I discover the church has a team, it does not take much coaxing to join the team. It does not matter that I am the oldest member on their roster. Many years have passed since I last donned a pair of skates and played this rough and tough game of games. Of course, we are in a church league, so no rough stuff allowed. But along the boards there are many questionable body checks. Just the same, I enjoy the outlet it provides and the exercise I need.

And then it happens! There is a scramble in front of the opponents' net. I have the puck and just when I am prepared to poke it into the net, I am bowled over. My right skate is jammed between sprawled bodies, and I am unable to yank it free. I feel the bone above my ankle give way, no matter how I resist. The weight of all the bodies is too great. When everyone has removed himself from on top of me, I am unable to stand to my feet. Is my ankle broken or just dislocated? Two players assist me to the bench. There my skate is removed. Swelling has already set in and I am in excruciating pain. They pray for me and play resumes.

I try to exercise my faith by standing on my feet, but the pain is just too much. A church member at the game remarks, "I guess if you were in Africa you would be healed by now." That really jolts me! Is it true what Dave just said? Why am I not healed here in Canada? Is God not the same anywhere you go? Prove it now, Lord, not only to me, but to my people here in Carstairs. Marion comes for me. She cannot believe what she sees. "I hope now you will quit hockey for sure!" she exclaims.

At home I attempt again to stand and walk. Is that not what Peter said: "In the Name of Jesus, stand up and walk"? It is no use. The pain is too severe. I am probably making it worse by standing on the leg. The ankle is swollen out of proportion, and there is a lump the size of a baseball above it. I end up on the floor, as the blankets on the bed only increased the pain as I tossed about keeping Marion awake at the same time. When morning finally arrives, I travel with Colleen to Olds, where she has a dental appointment. At the hospital they x-ray my leg and discover I have fractured my fibula bone. In fact, the broken ends have drifted apart from my putting weight on the leg when trying to stand.

The doctor forces the ends in place before setting the leg into a cast. When he does this I may have hit the ceiling had he not held onto me. It hurt that much! Colleen returns home without me as I am kept in the hospital for the night. In the morning he x-rays the fracture through the cast to see if it is set properly. All is well and he releases me from the hospital. I am to keep the cast on my leg for six to eight weeks, the doctor advises me. A pair of crutches are given to me so that I can get around. A fine mess I have gotten myself into. The man of faith hobbling about! Marion has come for me. It is Wednesday.

I have prepared a two-part message on faith. The first part I preached last Sunday. It was: "A person is literally what he thinks and believes." This Sunday is to be the climax. It is: "The Christian faith is not merely something we believe; it also involves what we confess." As I look at the sermon, I am tempted to lay it aside for a later date, as it just is not fitting right now. Why, just look at me! All the praying I have done has not brought healing. I have failed to be an example of someone who has confessed his faith and then is healed as a result.

The local press comes to our door and I am interviewed for an article in the paper. So now everyone knows that the pastor of the Church of God broke his leg while trying to score a goal. If there was anyone who did not know me before, he knows who I am now, for the photo on the front page is of me sitting on my favorite chair with a cast on my leg!

Sunday morning finds me behind the pulpit with the crutches leaning against it. I preach the second part of my message on faith. Yes, the devil tried to talk me out of it, but I managed to shake him off my back. I could not desert my post. I will go through with it even if I have not been the example thus far of someone who believes in miracles. I am soon caught up in the message. Before I realize it, I have said, "The next time you see me behind this pulpit, I will not be using these crutches!" During the closing song, the impact of what I just said suddenly hits me! Oh no, why did I have to say that? It is tough enough already. Why make it worse!

I pray more earnestly with much soul-searching and shedding of tears as the days keep passing by and no sign of any healing taking place. It is Thursday and Tim is flying in from Toronto to visit Colleen. It is a midnight flight, so Marion takes Colleen to pick him up at the Calgary airport. It is now ten days since I had the accident. Lying there on my bed, I continue searching for anything that may still be staying the hand of the Lord. I have only two more days left and then it is Sunday! "Lord, heal me," I keep praying.

Then it happens! A charge, like an electrical shock, enters the top of my head, continues through my body, and then passes along my right leg before exiting. There is no mistake about it! I finally receive the healing I have been waiting for. Praise the Lord! Hallelujah! I am ecstatic. Marion, Colleen, and Tim arrive soon after and I share the exciting news. I can still feel the glow of His touch.

In the morning I walk about without crutches, a difficult feat because of the metal heel on the cast. So I plan a trip to Olds and have the doctor remove my cast. But when I slide behind the wheel of the vehicle, which I had not done since that fateful night, my cast cracks all the way around right above my ankle just as I reach for the gas pedal! I wobble back into the house; the bottom part is now separate from the rest of the cast. It is like trying to walk in one high-heeled shoe. There is no pain in spite of walking in this awkward way. A real test that healing has taken place!

We decide to remove the cast ourselves and save the trip to Olds. Marion digs out the saw and we cut away the cast that I was to have worn for at least five more weeks. My foot feels fine and I walk into church two days later without crutches and testify of my healing. When I finally see the doctor, I explain to him what happened. He makes no comment, examining the foot and then saying that all is well. I can go home.

Now, why did God not heal my leg back at the arena? Why did He wait ten days to do it? I believe He wanted as many as possible to see this miraculous healing. Had it taken place at the hockey game, then my teammates may have thought it was only a sprain I had sustained. Nothing great about that! But He waited until I had appeared in the newspaper and before the congregation that first Sunday with a broken leg in a cast. There was no question about it now.

As well, it was a test of my faith. Would I preach the second part of my message on faith? And when I did, He had me proclaim that I would be healed by the following Sunday. It was now a time for me to go through a spiritual cleansing, spending hours studying the Word to build up my faith. Looking back, I can see that He healed me when the proper time had come. All I had to do was persevere.

Once settled in Carstairs, Marion tries to enroll in nursing school at Calgary but discovers there is a long waiting list ahead of her. So she resigns herself to being a pastor's wife, a role that she succeeds in very well. Women who come to Marion for counselling find Christ before they leave. She continues to experience healings in her own life here in Canada as well. Whenever she is stricken, a verse she likes to use is: "Though He slay me, yet will I trust Him" (Job 13:15).

Marion believes God also cares about the little things in our lives. While still in Anderson, during our furlough, the clothesdrier often quit working on her. I am away itinerating, so she called the repairman to fix it. This he did and hands her a bill for forty-five dollars. At the next washing the machine did the same thing, but this time she was not about to spend that amount again. Instead, she laid her hands on the drier and prayed. The machine promptly began to work! She had a similar experience with the sewing machine. After trying for an hour to fix it so that it would start sewing again, she gave up, laid hands on it, and prayed. When she tried it, the machine worked!

There are numerous miracles that take place at Carstairs, such as rebuking the rain clouds so that we can hold our baptismal service in which a woman in her seventies, whom Marion had led to the Lord, could be baptized along with Karen, Kirk's wife, and others. The rain is stayed until we are on our way home. Again, when it appeared that rain would interfere with the church Sunday school picnic, I take the assistant pastor with me and we command the rain to stay away until the functions have ended. Dark clouds are everywhere, but it does not rain. Praise the Lord!

I can hear some of you saying right about now, "Sure, sure, it probably would not have rained anyway." That may be so. But what I am sure of is that rain was predicted and all signs showed that it would rain, and then it did not! I choose, therefore, to credit Him for this miracle.

Then, there is the time hail is forecast and sure enough, we can see it coming. I stand out on our back veranda and command the angry clouds to pass us by. They churn, roll, and butt as if against an invisible wall. In the end they fail to reach our place and rumble on by. I felt a fury lashing out at me from those raging clouds as I have never felt before from the powers of nature. But I knew I was in the right. Did not

Jesus still the storm? And then scold the disciples for not having the faith to do it for themselves? (Luke 8: 22–25).

I could go on mentioning other occasions where I felt God as real here in America as back in Africa. If I at any time felt that I had left Him in the mission field, I soon learned that He is wherever we are. All we need to do is believe. His power is the same. How grateful I am for that.

Will Marion and I ever see Him work miracles in Africa again? Will we ever set foot on that continent once more? To make fresh tracks in a new land where Christ is needed? Where to next? I dare not let my heart run away just yet, but the time may come when I will answer the call to return to my beloved Africa.

We are living a good life here in Canada. I drive a beautiful car over smooth highways. Our home is comfortable. The walls in the den are decorated with trophies and artifacts from Africa. Many of our evenings are spent reminiscing of our adventures in Tanzania and Kenya. Mark is still in high school, but Colleen is married and so is Kirk, both to missionary kids they met in Africa (Colleen to Timothy Stevenson and Kirk to Karen McLain).

No wonder, then, that our conversation, during our family gatherings, turns to that place we called home for so many years. Those are years we will never forget. Someone has said, "Once Africa digs her claws into you, she does not let go!" So very true.

(Author's Note: The book *Amid Perils Often* follows this one.)